SARUM USE

The Ancient Customs
of Salisbury

Illuminated page from the Missal of Henry of Chichester, Salisbury *c.*1250 (*John Rylands Library of Manchester*). The tonsured Henry in alb and cope is depicted kneeling before the Virgin and Child pleading 'Son of God have mercy on me'. The motifs are clearly those of the 13th-century Gothic style of the new cathedral.

SARUM USE
The Ancient Customs of Salisbury

Philip Baxter

Spire Books Ltd

PO Box 2336, Reading RG4 5WJ
www.spirebooks.com

Spire Books Ltd
PO Box 2336
Reading RG4 5WJ
www.spirebooks.com

CIP data:
A catalogue record for this book is available
from the British Library
ISBN 978-1-904965-18-3

Designed and produced by John Elliott
Text set in Bembo

Printed by Latimer Trend, Eastover Road, Plymouth

Cover illustration: Sherborne Missal: details from Easter Day. Bishop of Sarum with Abbot of Sherborne flanked by SS Peter and Paul with (below) Benedictine scribe John Whas and Dominican illuminator John Siferwas (*Duke of Northumberland and the British Library*).

CONTENTS

Dedicated to:

the Bishop of Salisbury, Dean and Chapter, musicians,
staff and voluntary workers of Salisbury Cathedral

Acknowledgements for
invaluable help and advice:

The Rt Revd David Stancliffe
The Rt Revd John Baker
The Rt Revd Martin Dudley
The Revd Canon Ian Dunlop
The Revd Canon Jeremy Davies
The Revd Canon David Baxter
Mr Stephen Baxter
The Revd John Cowdrey
Mrs Daphne Stroud

The cathedral from the north east.

FOREWORDS

From the Bishop of Salisbury

When Giles de Bridport wrote that 'among the churches of the whole world, the Church of Sarum hath shone resplendent, like the sunne in his full orb, in respect of its divine service and its ministers', he was speaking perhaps more prophetically than he knew.

Throughout the Middle Ages, the particular liturgical use of Salisbury which we know as the Sarum Rite increased in popularity, and indeed became the major use in pre-Reformation England. Like other regional uses, it gives a characteristically local feel to the Wessex Rite, and as Philip Baxter points out in his splendidly readable study, the Rite has continued to influence the whole style of English worship both in the *Book of Common Prayer* and in more recent revisions.

I hope that this colourful introduction to the history of the Rite's development will service both as a stimulus to those who wish to know more, and as a reminder to the more general reader that the Use of Sarum is, in its own way, as significant an artistic creation in the history of the mediaeval West as is the cathedral building itself.

From the Dean of Salisbury

Eamon Duffy in his magisterial and controversial account of traditional religion in England in the late Middle Ages *The Stripping of the Altars* writes

> any study of late mediaeval religion must begin with the liturgy, for within that great seasonal cycle of fast and festival, of ritual observance and symbolic gesture, lay Christians found the paradigms and the stories which shaped their perception of the world and their place in it. Within the liturgy: birth, copulation and death, journeying and homecoming, guilt and forgiveness, the blessing of homely things and the call to pass beyond them, were all located, tested and sanctioned. In the liturgy and in the sacramental celebration which were its central moments, mediaeval people found the key to the meaning and purpose of their lives.

The liturgy of the Church – its rites and ceremonies, its disciplines and devotions, its words and music – stretched out and touched the lives of men and women in the mediaeval world. It expressed for them, through its mystery as much as through its doctrines, the longings and aspirations of ordinary people for a world beyond the physical and the mundane. It is a world we find it difficult to imagine today. Even though we live in a city which is dominated by one of the greatest structures of the mediaeval religious mind; even when we live near to such a wonder as Salisbury Cathedral; even though indeed we may share often or from time to time in the liturgies which remain the daily offering of the people of God, today as they were 750 years ago: even with all these visual aids to encourage our religious imagination, it is difficult to get alongside the mindset of those for whom the sacred and the secular were bound inextricably together. Life and the living of it, not to mention death and the dying of it, was bound by religious preoccupations.

So liturgy in late mediaeval times was the clue to understanding the mediaeval mindset. And where better to understand the liturgy than here in Salisbury, where a liturgical pattern established itself in the wake of the Norman conquest that became formalised, elaborated and codified in the 13th century and endured as the most widely used liturgical observance in England until the Reformation – let us say until Thomas Cranmer's groundbreaking liturgies in English of 1549 and 1552, which became the basis for the *Book of Common Prayer* in 1662. And even Cranmer's drastic revisions, while they owed much to the theology of the German reformers, also drew on the ancient liturgical use of the English – The Sarum Use.

As Diarmaid McCulloch writes in his biography of Thomas Cranmer:

> At the heart of Cranmer's 1549 Eucharistic Rite was a prayer of consecration, which revealed the prayer's kinship with the Sarum version of the Canon of the Mass, which he had probably taken at the beginning of his work on the Eucharist and translated into English. Even after modification, the Sarum Canon still provided much of the prayer's framework.

So, even though the Mass in Latin more or less ended at the Reformation in England, the influence of the Sarum Use continued to pervade the public worship of the reformers.

It is into that tradition of liturgical excellence, mediated to us through Archbishop Thomas Cranmer, that we in Salisbury feel we have entered. The reprinting of Philip Baxter's excellent introduction to the Sarum Use reminds us of the meticulous attention to detail in the elaboration of worship that was part of the Salisbury tradition and recalls us today to the centrality of worship in the life of the Cathedral. And even though our contemporary mindset is not as preoccupied with religious and liturgical issues as it once was, nevertheless the Christian commitment to worship is the point at which we begin most profitably to engage with the issues of religious controversy that still divide our world. Philip Baxter's book is a timely bringing together of our past and our present as we celebrate the 750th anniversary of the consecration of Salisbury Cathedral.

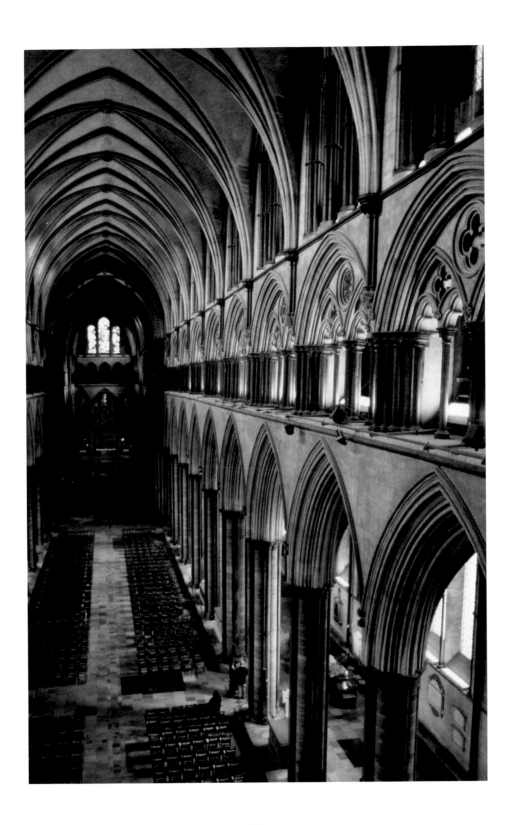

INTRODUCTION

The first edition of this book was published in 1992, to celebrate the 900th anniversary of the dedication of the first cathedral at Old Sarum. This second edition in 2008 marks the 750th anniversary of the dedication of the new cathedral on 30th September 1258. Between those celebrated years of 1092 and 1258, there developed a highly-complex code of customs, both managerial and liturgical, based on traditions rooted in Anglo-Saxon Sherborne, themselves influenced by Celtic and early continental practice, and with newer influences from the Church in Normandy. Those customs also were up-dated, refined and recorded over the following three centuries.

The Sarum Use is often referred to, rather too narrowly, as the Sarum Rite. This indicates that ritual is the sole subject, but in fact it was the business and managerial aspects of the first cathedral foundation at (Old) Sarum which were the initial attraction to the many other Norman cathedral chapters then being established. This initial guidance regarding staffing, duties, property-ownership, prebendal and financial organisation was provided by the first two outstanding administrator-bishops, Osmund and Roger. Later bishops, notably Jocelin, in the later years at (Old) Sarum, and Richard Poore, at the foundation of New Sarum, produced valuable records on liturgical customs, these being of increasing attraction since Sarum's establishment, and especially since the no doubt glorious ceremonial of the well-attended dedication of 1258.

The overall success of Sarum was due to many factors, not least the interface of Church and State in terms of personalities and politics, but very largely to the professional approach to literature and music which bishops, deans and chapters successively applied to their daily worship. It is comforting to realise that the same professionalism pertains today, to which this book is dedicated.

Philip Baxter
4 December 2007. Deposition (burial) of Osmund (1099).

1

EARLY BRITISH LITURGY

The first Christian religious practices in Britain are thought to have filtered through the channels of the Roman Empire by the late second century. The Venerable Bede mentions the pope's having sent two bishops to Britain in AD 180, and Tertullian mentions the Church in 208. *Crockford's Clerical Directory* lists eleven bishops of London before Restitutus in 314. If they averaged an episcopacy of twelve years each, that would point to a first bishop of London around 180, thus supporting Bede and Tertullian. It is known there were bishops from Britain at the first Christian Council of Arles in 314, probably representing the urban communities of London and York, and possibly also Lincoln and Cirencester. No records survive to indicate details of ecclesiastical organisation or liturgical use. It is most likely that what liturgy was written down would have been common to that in Roman Gaul.

By the early fifth century, the end of the Roman occupation resulted in the penetration of southern, eastern and middle Britain by the incoming Saxons, Jutes and Angles, and in the destruction or suppression of the organised Christian church in these regions. Only in the remoter parts of the north and west, away from the invaders' stepping-stone of the south-east, did the church prevail in its British-Celtic form.

The fifth century saw missions to the more receptive Celts, including those of Ninian to Scotland, and Patrick to Ireland, as well as others, from the western, Celtic area of Gaul. Thus, the newly-flourishing Gallican Use, and perhaps its Mozarabic variant in Spain, influenced liturgical use in Britain. By the sixth century, when David continued the spread of Christianity in Wales, and Columba from Iona to Scotland, the Celtic traditions were at their zenith.

The rest of Britain was still largely in its lapsed heathen state when Pope Gregory, at the end of the sixth century, heard of the marriage of the king of Kent to a Christian Frankish princess. He saw this as a great opportunity to re-Christianise Britain, and sent the prior of his own monastery in Rome, Augustine, with an entourage of monks, to re-establish the bishoprics of London and York in Britain's two main cities.

Extract from Easter Day Mass, an illuminated page from the missal of Sir Richard Sutton, (*Principal and Fellows of Brasenose College, Oxford*).

After much fear and doubting en route, Augustine was welcomed to the Canterbury court in 597. Unfortunately, the political climate outside Kent caused difficulties to the mission, and Augustine withdrew. He retired to the relative comfort of Canterbury, thus establishing there, by default, the cradle of future Christianity in Britain. The Rochester and London bishoprics did soon follow, but Augustine consecrated others to continue the mission.

Even where the church already existed, in the west of Britain, Augustine met with disagreement, though perhaps more liturgical than doctrinal. Augustine's practices were up-to-date Rome-based, where the British-Celtic church, more independent, more artistically-flamboyant, and long out of kilter with Rome, had never followed promulgations from Rome, and even followed the old, unamended calendar. The two sides even disagreed on the date of the all-important Easter celebrations.

The post-Augustine bishops realised that a united church was essential for the general progress of Christianity, and a solution of the differences was sought. In 664, the bishops and principals of both parties met at a synod at Hilda's new abbey at Whitby.[1] It didn't agree on everything, but it did declare the universal adoption of the up-dated Roman calendar. A gradual move towards general observance of the Roman liturgy then followed, supported by key churchmen who had both a background of Celtic traditions and up-to-date Roman education. These included Bishop Wilfred of York, who had been used to the old ways at Ripon but had been educated at Canterbury and Rome; Archbishop Theodore of Canterbury, who had been born into the Eastern church at Tarsus, which had fed ideas through the Milanese, Gallican and Mozarabic uses to the western Celtic church; and Bishop Aldhelm of Sherborne, who had been brought up with the British Celtic-Anglo-Saxon traditions of western Britain (whose seeds of difference flowered into a Sherborne, then Sarum Use), but was a scholar and colleague of Theodore. These important views balanced the more robust Celtic adherences of Bishops Chad of Lichfield and Cuthbert of Durham who were determined not to lose all their beloved customs. There was, therefore, more of a fusion of rites than an eclipse of one by the other.

A further boost to the Roman cause in the Celtic north came with the visit to the monastery of Jarrow-Wearmouth, and almost certainly to the Saxon minster at York, by John the Archcantor or Precentor of the papal court in Rome. The exact Gregorian plainsong was thus passed on, first-hand, to the British church. At the Synod of Clovesho in 747, it was laid down:

> that in one and the same manner, we all celebrate the Sacred Festivals … in our celebration of Mass, and in our manner of singing; all has to be done according to the pattern which we have received in writing from the Roman Church.[2]

The British-Celtic Use was thus, at least officially, abandoned, and the Roman Use promoted.

2

SHERBORNE AND RAMSBURY

In 705, the King of Wessex subdivided his kingdom's bishopric, centred on Winchester, to form a second bishopric to cover the western half of the kingdom, later to become Wiltshire, Dorset, Somerset, Devon and Cornwall. Aldhelm, then Abbot of Malmesbury, and a kinsman of King Ine, was appointed bishop of the new see, centred on a monastic cathedral at Sherborne. Aldhelm was the earliest British scholar to achieve fame, being a generation older than the Venerable Bede.[3] He was first taught by an Irish scholar, and then by Hadrian the Abbot, and Theodore the Archbishop, at Canterbury. He has been described as 'beyond comparison the most learned and ingenious western scholar of the late seventh century.'[4]

Through generous royal patronage, and the reputation of its scholarly and saintly protobishop, Sherborne gathered considerable prestige. It was the location of the cathedral and mother church of the marginal southern Celtic races, and yet at the centre of the unifying force of Saxon kings whose power and organisation moulded the one kingdom of England. Doubtless, then, much attention and patronage was paid to its foundation, organisation, customs and liturgy.

The rich religious traditions of this Celtic area, and its Anglo-Saxon influences, would have been recognised and absorbed into the early cathedral's practices. Of the latter were the abundant use of candles, around the altar on high candlesticks, over the altar or presbytery on a large, multi-ring corona, and portable candles carried by all at such as Candlemass (the feast of the Purification of the Blessed Virgin Mary). As at baptism, a personal sign of the cross in dedication was made on Ash Wednesday, with ash from the burnt palm leaves of the previous Palm Sunday. The sign of the cross on documents was then not an indication of illiteracy, as now, but a sign of Christian faith, dedication and promise to the statements made. Seals with coats of arms or symbols, for the same purpose, were brought in later by the Normans.

It is likely that a school for boys was an integral part of the Sherborne foundation (girls of similar status went to convents such as Amesbury, Shaftesbury and Wilton). Bishop Aldhelm was commonly regarded as one of the country's leaders of the intellectual and artistic movement. As he was a renowned teacher, musician and artist, there is little doubt there would have been an educational centre, at the very least to maintain a good standard of liturgy and musicianship in the cathedral.

King Alfred the Great (849–899) was also renowned as a scholar, writer and promoter of education. That he and his three brothers, all of whom preceded him as king, were brought up and taught at Sherborne might be understood from the burial of two of them in the cathedral.

It is believed that a community of secular canons may have served the cathedral at some later time, but it was officially converted in 998 to a Benedictine abbey, following the monastic bias of the episcopacy at that time and the bishop of the see was concurrently abbot of the monastery. This change in organisation caused a change in liturgical practice and in other aspects of the residents' lives, as Benedictine houses were duty-bound to follow the Benedictine Rule.

Ramsbury became the centre of another subdivision of Wessex in 909, when Wiltshire and Berkshire became a separate bishopric. Athelstan was the first bishop, and again, though possibly secular, the diocesan community there may have been run on quasi-monastic lines. In 1045, Herman was appointed bishop. He was the son of a Flemish prince, and formerly Chaplain to King Edward the Confessor. When the house of Godwin, Earl of Essex, proved disloyal to Edward, causing considerable trouble in the area, Herman had to flee from Ramsbury, and returned to a monastery at St Omer near Calais. This would point to Herman's experience as essentially monastic.

The see of Ramsbury was not large, in relative terms, and despite having Windsor in its bounds, there was at that time no royal castle or other benefits to bring wealth to the see. Being on the Wessex boundary with Mercia, it had suffered plundering during many wars, some involving Danish invaders. When peace eventually came back to Wessex, Edward decided to amalgamate the impoverished see of Ramsbury with the flourishing one of Sherborne. Edward saw Herman as the ideal, experienced abbot-bishop to head the extended see, and appointed him to that post in 1058.

For seventeen more years, Herman guided a successful monastic cathedral at Sherborne, preserving its rich heritage of traditions and customs, its literature, art and music. The Norman

Conquest did not disturb either bishop or organisation, especially as Herman was of continental descent, but King William's Council of London in 1075 directed that cathedrals and their diocesan buildings and personnel should be centred in fortified towns rather than open market towns. The vast see from Windsor to Cornwall was to be centred in the fortified, former Bishop of Ramsbury's manor, on the hill of Sarisberie.

Ramsbury continued as a parish church, and Sherborne continued as an abbey until the dissolution of the greater monasteries in 1539/40 when it also became a parish church.

3

OLD SARUM

The Normans re-fortified the ancient Iron Age hill for new occupation. William's early experience following the Conquest, more especially in the north, was such that powerful subjugation of the country was necessary through a small but very select body of barons and bishops, with castles and fortifications to protect them and to show a strong face of government to the populace. In this respect, Old Sarum was ideal. The very first function here was the paying off of the Conquest army in 1077. Some soldiers complained that they had suffered particularly bad conditions and deserved more. William, almost in biblical style, made them wait another forty days before being paid, at the same level!

It might be convenient here to explain the origin of the name 'Sarum.' In medieval documents, the language was normally Latin. The town of Sarisburgh or Sarisberie was thus Latinised as Sarisberiense, but it was usual for scribes to shorten long words, for obvious reasons, and put a line over the shortened area. The line eventually developed into an apostrophe, thus, in such as the Magna Carta, William Longspee is referred to as the Count of Sar' (short for Sarisberiense). This short name was commonly used until, to give it a more credible sound, the common Latin town ending of 'um' was added, making it Sar'um.

Herman remained as bishop and moved in to Old Sarum with his archdeacons to build a cathedral, probably on the site of a Saxon manorial church, dedicating it to the Blessed Virgin Mary, as was Sherborne. Almost certainly, as former monks at Sherborne, they would have started a monastic community at Old Sarum,[5] placing their cloister, again indicating monastic design, unusually, on the north side, for reasons of better privacy, away from the view of the higher, castle buildings. It is also fairly certain that they brought with them their liturgical books and practices, thus giving continuity to the long heritage of Celtic-Saxon customs.

One notable member of the first monastic community at Old Sarum was Goscelin. He was a scholar and author who had travelled with Herman from St Omer to Rome and back to Sherborne. That he didn't settle into the new, secular regime after Herman, points again to the initial foundation as being monastic. Goscelin went on to Canterbury and settled into the monastic community there.

Herman made a distinguished start to the Sarum story and, unlike many of his contemporary Anglo-Saxon bishop colleagues, was favoured by King William because of his continental royal origin. Sadly, he survived only three more years, which may indicate the harsh physical conditions of establishing a new community up on the hill.

William then had the opportunity to choose a new bishop for his own domestic diocese, as Clarendon palace, only two or three miles away, set up by Saxon kings as a hunting lodge near to the Wessex shire capital of Wilton, became the Norman kings' chief English home. Two reasons for this were its nearness to the ports of Poole, Christchurch and Southampton for sailing to Normandy, and its proximity to the New Forest hunting ground. William needed not only a bishop, but a personal confessor and adviser. Utmost loyalty and strongest management ability were vital to helping William govern the country.

William's choice of domestic bishop was an easy one. His kinsman, Osmund, as a chief administrator in Normandy and then Chancellor of England, was the ideal, able and trustworthy man. However, Osmund's background was not monastic, and he decided that Sarisburie's cathedral community should be one of secular canons, who nevertheless shared a common life with common meals adjacent to the cathedral. He gave much of his land and income, all of which had been given to him by William, to the establishment of prebends to support this chapter of canons.

This appointment proved to be most successful and a major feature in bringing Sarum and its organisation into extraordinary prominence. Being a reasonable, diplomatic and much-loved bishop, and unlike many other dictatorial and brutal barons, he took his time in making changes, and carried his colleagues with him. An important factor contributing to the slow but positive change was the building programme of the new cathedral, started by Herman, and which must have disrupted the stability of any pattern of life first established there. Osmund patiently endured an unsettled but exciting initial twelve years.

One of Osmund's major national tasks was, in 1086, to organise at Sarum a magnificent and unique event, possibly as grand as William's coronation. The Council of Sarum was held to receive the report of the Domesday survey, along with the fealty of the barons, bishops and major land holders to the king.[6] It may be idle, but nevertheless fascinating to speculate how the gathering of perhaps 800 or more noblemen housed: the two archbishops probably with Osmund in Sarum's central castle; the other dozen or so bishops with the canons in the cathedral houses; the barons with the king at Clarendon, and lesser nobles in the inns and merchants' houses in Sarum town.

The organisation of the liturgy and choreography of the

Extract from the 1086 Domesday Book listing landholders in Wiltshire. Heading the list are King William and the bishops of Winchester and Salisbury.

event in the cathedral would have doubtless impressed all present. Although the cathedral was not quite finished, this was the start of big impressions and renown from Sarum. The king was delighted with the event:

> There, his counsellors came to him, and all men who were holding land that were of worth from all over England, whosoever's vassals they were. They all bowed to him and were his vassals, and swore him oaths of loyalty that they would, against all other men, be loyal to him.

It was William's final show of power; a grand finale to the Conquest. The transformation of the state and church was virtually complete, in a now relatively peaceful country. He had replaced some four thousand Anglo-Saxon thegns with two hundred Norman barons, and knew all their property holdings. Immediately following the council, William left a relatively peaceful England for a still-disturbed and warring Normandy, where he died the following year.

It is interesting to reflect that although the pope had given a pre-Conquest blessing to William for a peaceful bid to the English throne, he had not condoned war, and penances were given to all soldiers who had killed anyone. William himself had been obliged to build an abbey in Caen, where, in the end, he himself was laid to rest.

Osmund continued his noble work, and initiated a scriptorium, he himself writing some of the first generation Norman documents for the cathedral organisation. His chief work was the *Carta* or Charter, laying down the constitution of the foundation and its management and financial bases. This was influenced by Norman patterns, though no firm standard had yet evolved.

In 1091 King William II met with his barons and bishops at Hastings, twenty-five years after his father's historic victory. Osmund attended and took there, for official signing and sealing, his *Carta* for the newly completed cathedral. The cathedral was dedicated on 5 April 1092, and Osmund's constitutional organisation took effect.

Opposite: Old Sarum showing the foundations of the cathedral and the remains of the Castle. Herman's and Osmund's original is the small central plan with apsidal chapels. Roger extended this on all four sides providing an eastern ambulatory for the early processions, and a chapter house off the north transept (*Salisbury Newspapers Ltd*).

23

The charter, surviving in later copies of it, made provision for a small hierarchy of senior clergy, including a dean as second senior after the bishop (who at this time was central and permanent in the cathedral's operation), and three archdeacons for diocesan management, there being one each for Berkshire, Dorset and Wiltshire. Osmund gave endowments from his own estates to support a communal chapter of some thirty to thirty-six prebendal canons. (A canon, Latin: *canonicus*, was a person living, usually communally, under canons or statutes. A prebend was the income from a manor or parcel of land allocated to a canon for his subsistence.)

Uniquely in cathedral constitutions, Osmund appointed himself a canon amongst canons, with a share of prebendal income, probably that of *Major pars altaris*; the major part of offerings at the altar. He thus sat as a full member of the chapter, over which he also presided.[8]

The bishop's throne was set in principal in the eastern apse of the sanctuary, facing west. The dean, as next senior, sat on the bishop's right (north side) and the archdeacons arrayed in the apsidal semi-circle, all facing west across the altar to the main body of canons in a closed quire. (In monastic foundations, the arrangement was similar, with the abbot as central, and the priest monks in a closed quire.) This was the normal Romanesque pattern of church design originating in the pattern for the Roman civic forum, where the civil service hierarchy stood on a platform in an apse facing the people across the table.

Up to Anglo-Saxon, and possibly early Norman times, there were neither candles nor cross on the altar, but candles, essentially for light as well as symbolism, were placed around the altar. On a beam over the altar were placed holy relics. The beam was supported by two pillars, a remnant from the early church tradition of four pillars bearing a canopy over the altar, in turn reflecting the Jewish Temple's Holy of Holies. Hanging over the altar was a silver pyx for the reserved sacrament, always to be available for the sick whether of the community or pilgrim visitor. In front of the altar hung a corona or chandelier of candles.

The quire, for the canons and other clergy, was enclosed by seven foot walls and a quire screen. The height of these increased over succeeding stages of design. The point was that the religious community was blatantly a class apart from the townspeople. The latter simply stood in the nave, unable to see the action of the Mass, other than the gospel on the pulpitum. Theirs was to attend, not to participate.

Osmund's episcopacy lasted almost to the end of the reign of his cousin, William Rufus, totalling twenty-one years at (Old) Sarum. During that time he had completed the first cathedral, established a chartered organisation, and built upon previous customs with his own ideas, probably influenced by practices at the cathedral of Normandy's capital, Rouen, which he would have known well. Notwithstanding his *Carta*, there is no evidence of a full, written Consuetudinary or Customary at this time, although a later one credits Osmund with such initiation.

Osmund's highly esteemed administration was a tradition in itself and undoubtedly a firm foundation for Sarum's renown. His body was (first) deposited at Old Sarum on 4 December 1099, and efforts began immediately to seek canonisation (sainthood) for him.

Osmund's successor, under a new king, Henry I, was not consecrated for another eight years. The normal episcopal benefits and rights of income were claimed by the king during this time, which in turn discouraged him from making a hasty appointment. The interregnum may have caused difficulties and even malpractices in the far reaches of the diocese where hard-pressed archdeacons visited less frequently. However, the cathedral was better placed in that Osmund's charter provided some independent security for the chapter aided by former episcopal lands, and there was an established hierarchy of clergy to control the organisation. The greatest need for direction and support was in the repair and rebuilding of the fabric, for soon after the completion celebrations of 1092, there was a collapse of the structure.

Roger of Caen was consecrated bishop in 1107, having risen, through ability, from humble Norman stock to a proven and respected legal and financial administrator in the Court of Normandy, and thence to Chancellor and Justiciar of England. It was under Roger's direction that a chequered cloth or board was initiated to facilitate accounting of the king's dues from his lands and other landowners. The Chancellor's Exchequer was so named from this function.

Bishop Roger proceeded to build on Osmund's great work, extending the cathedral in all four directions. He built a western porch, extended the north and south transepts, and added an ambulatory and chapelled east end. His increasing power and wealth, and his Norman-bred ambition, led him to build castles at Malmesbury, Devizes and Sherborne, and to rebuild the castle in grander style at Sarum, formerly held by Osmund as Earl of Dorset, and now providing lavish accommodation for himself. It was now officially the bishop's palace. These external comforts also indicated how remote he was becoming from the day-to-day running of the cathedral.

Like Osmund he was not a monastic, and in 1122 he resigned his incongruous holding of the Abbacy of Sherborne, hitherto from pre-Sarum days an ex-officio title with the bishopric, in order to take on higher responsibility, concurrent with his bishopric, as chief minister and vice-regent to the King.

Proximity to the royal palace at Clarendon again facilitated this royal and national work, and Roger increased his power and esteem throughout the country. His supreme loyalty and ability had taken him to the position of deputy king, which meant that when the king was away in Normandy, as was often the case and for long periods, England was effectively ruled from Sarum. It is not surprising, then, that in matters ecclesiastical and liturgical, as well as legal and financial, Sarum was considered the ultimate authority, and that what was decreed for use at Sarum, was good enough for anyone.

In 1123, King Henry allowed Roger a leading role in the nomination of a new Archbishop of Canterbury. (Roger himself would not want the job as he was much closer to the king at Sarum.) Roger declared that he would not support a monk in that office, but that a secular canon be preferred to head a secular church. Roger's view was not entirely welcomed. It was said:

> The prior and monks of Canterbury and all others who were monks in orders spoke against it for fully two days, but it availed them nothing, for the Bishop of Sarum was strong and ruled all England ... [9]

A papal legate declared it illegal 'that a secular cleric should be set over monks'. Nevertheless, 'the king would not undo it for love of the Bishop of Sarum.'

His elevation to vice-regal duties required Roger to delegate even more authority and responsibility to the cathedral hierarchy. Hitherto, the centrality of the bishop to the organisation and worship of the cathedral was facilitated by his regular presence. This had been the norm and was still the norm in other

Extract from *St Osmund's Register*. Vetus Reg(ist)rum refers to Old Register, probably Osmund's, but this is a revision by Richard Poore in the 13th century. (*Diocesan Records Office: WRO D1/1/1*) The paragraph beginning "Quantuor itaque sunt persone principales in ecclesia Sar': Decani, Cantor, Cancellarius, Thesaurius & iii archidiaconi videlicte archidiaconus Dorsete, Berchesirie & duo Wiltesire preterea subdiaconus, succentor" translates: There are then four principal persons in Sarum church: dean, precentor, chancellor, treasurer and four archdeacons namely the archdeacons of Dorset, Berkshire and two for Wiltshire also being sub-dean and succentor.

cathedrals, but it could not continue at Sarum with Roger's frequent absences on state duties.

Roger further strengthened the hierarchy by formalising the post of chief scholar, concerned with education and the library of manuscripts, into that of cathedral canon chancellor, creating also the posts of precentor and treasurer. This secured the *quadumvirate* of dignitaries to control the whole business and worship of the cathedral from then on. The dean (Latin: *decanus* = titular head, of a body of ten) was the senior, and thus now head of the cathedral. The precentor (Latin: *praecantor* = prime singer) taught and supervised the music of the services. The chancellor (Latin: *cancellarius* = secretary or administrator) controlled the business of the chapter, the library and the education of boys in the cathedral school. The treasurer (Latin: *thesaurus* = treasure or valuables) supervised vestments, eucharistic vessels, statues, ornaments, pictures, candles, incense, wine, and the building itself and its funds.

In order to confirm the individual security of the dignitaries, and the canons at the next level of hierarchy, Roger allocated properties from his own accumulated estate for individual prebends as opposed to communal ones. Furthering Osmund's endowment precedent, Roger allocated himself a prebend (Potterne, on the way to his Devizes castle) and established the bishop's place in chapter as a canon among canons but not as president. This arrangement was not necessary at other cathedrals, and was not widely followed, but it was virtually essential at Sarum where the cathedral had to proceed independently of its regal and stately bishop.

In his greatly extended quire, Roger made some radical alterations. With his central presence now redundant, the semi-circular formation of west-facing clergy was also redundant, so the new east end was not of the Romanesque apsidal pattern but virtually square, the three chapels not radiating but squarely facing east. With ample room in the quire, all clergy were now in one body, with the bishop's throne moved to the nearest point on the west side of the altar for convenience when he was present, and the four principals at the four corners of the body of clergy.

The major liturgical change which this arrangement effected was that, after the best part of a millennium of west-facing celebrations at the altar, they were now east-facing. The celebrant's right hand was now on the south side, not the north. This dictated the senior side for positioning both bishop and dean. Others, as before, were arrayed on the two sides, the prebendal canons at the high back, with minor canons and priests in the middle, and deacons, acolytes and boys in the lower front.

The east end was considered no longer appropriate for chapter meetings, and a custom-built chapter house was the obvious development. Just as today's meetings often begin with prayer, so the chapter meetings at that time, even in a separate chapter house, included the chapter mass. Again, the chief position in the chapter house seating arrangements was for the dean as president. The bishop, if present, took a seat as a canon.

Whilst it remained the prerogative of the bishop to choose, out of his diocesan clergy, members for promotion to canon, it was for the dean and chapter, as owner of the prebends, to allocate a particular prebend to the chosen canon, and to perform the ritual installation of the canon to that particular prebendal stall in the quire.

Roger was bishop for a glorious episcopacy of thirty-two years, and it could be said that the status and stability achieved in Sarum's first fifty years under two illustrious bishops were the foundation of Sarum's growing renown over the next century and more. The less welcome development for Roger, was the death of King Henry in 1135, and the following struggle for the crown. He made a vain attempt at the impossible dual task of pleasing both sides of the struggle. He first backed Matilda then changed sides when Stephen proved the stronger. Stephen was less than pleased with this, and furthermore was probably very jealous of the power Roger had over the church and even the land. Roger was deposed, disqualified from clerical office and imprisoned.

Stephen's love of castles rose above his love of bishops and cathedrals, and he seized Sarum castle for his own, confiscating all the amassed wealth he found there. He founded a new church for the Sarum community, separate from the cathedral and episcopal jurisdiction, the Chapel Royal of the Holy Cross. He also founded a new priory at Ivychurch on his Clarendon estate; this was no doubt his 'safer' contribution to the Crusades, the first of which had already claimed the life of his father. Both these foundations out-survived Stephen, but Roger did not. He died a destitute and broken man four years later in 1139. It was a sad end for such a notable and talented, if ambitious and worldly, bishop-baron.

The next bishop in office, Jocelin de Bohun, had to be content outside the castle in a new bishop's residence to the north-east of the cathedral and cloister. This separation of castle and cathedral was the beginning of worsening relationships which affected the canons over the following fifty or sixty years. The military never forgot that they had been given the upper hand in the control of Sarum town at the expense of the bishop. Stephen did not trust another bishop of Sarum with high civil office, but conversely, Jocelin was able to devote his full capabilities to the cathedral and his diocese.

Jocelin strengthened the chapter, creating further individual prebends and extending the hierarchy to allow for management by delegation. Under the four principals, he appointed four assistants from the chapter for deputising duties. These were the sub-dean, succentor, vice-chancellor and sub-treasurer. The canons were responsible for staffing the many services each day, sitting in their stalls to sing the vast quantity of psalms and antiphons of the office, and the whole psalter was sung through in full every week, or saying mass at one of the many altars. They would also make priestly visits to those parishes where they held their prebend, to minister to the people, support and pay their appointed vicar who held services, vicariousy on their behalf, and, of course, to collect their income, either in cash or in kind. Prebendary canons were doubly fortunate in having these parochial rights (from which comes the word rector) as well as, when present, a share in the cathedral *communa*, the free provision of food and necessities shared by those actually resident in the close. Prebends were not hereditary, but owned by the cathedral chapter, and held in trust for the time being by the canon appointed by the bishop or sometimes king or even pope. The origins of the prebendal properties were various. Some were church tithes and rights, some were whole manors, and some were just an odd farm or field. They came out of episcopal holdings or were given by donors, anywhere, to the cathedral out of generosity, penance or for the securing of a peaceful spirit, in this world or the next. This accounts for some prebends being outside the diocese, such as the chancellor's Bricklesworth prebend.

The Sherborne prebend was traditionally held by the abbot of Sherborne Abbey, who was thereby a canon and a member of the chapter. The house at the west end of the Close was for his use, and is now the Salisbury and Wiltshire Museum. The prebend was awarded to the abbot in return for the abbey's gift to the dean and chapter of the churches of Lyme and Halstock, and other benefits. The French abbots of Saint Wandrille, Bec and Montebourg, in Normandy were awarded the prebends of Upavon, Ogbourne and Loders respectively, in return for those several monastic cell churches in the diocese hitherto held by them.[10] All three abbots were assigned prebendal stalls in the quire, and places in chapter, but were exempt from residence on their agreement to maintain vicars-choral to perform their duties vicariously.

The matured prebendal arrangements, along with precedents of other customs were probably written, along with his own management ideas, by Jocelin into an *Institutio*, once believed to have been originated by Osmund. Jocelin, himself permanently resident, also recorded rules and traditions regarding residence and share of the *communa*.

There was one episode of considerable notoriety in the middle of Jocelin's episcopacy, when Henry II attempted to minimise the power of the Church, and particularly the power of the pope within his kingdom. The royal palace at Clarendon, enlarged and much used by Henry, was the venue in January 1164 for all English bishops to consider Henry's draft of a charter to empower his civil courts of justice to apply to clergy as well as laity, and to prevent the clergy's recourse to Rome, where they invariably enjoyed more lenient justice. These proposals to give Henry greater control of the Church, became known as the Constitutions of Clarendon. During this council, attended also by barons and other magnates, presumably to give Henry substantial moral support, the bishops were ready to concede to the king's wishes.

However, Thomas Becket, promoted to Archbishop of Canterbury by Henry, saw in the Constitutions an eroding of the Church's rights and influence in the lives of clergy, and refused to append his signature to the document. His contempt on the issue, in the public face of Henry, aggravated the friction between them. This led, through a combination of causes, to Becket's excommunicating Henry and his ally Jocelin of Sarum. For the sake of his life, Becket went into exile to Pontigny Abbey, returning in December 1170 only to be martyred in his own cathedral at Canterbury. Such was the shock to the western Church at this profane fatality that Becket was canonised within a record three years.

Bishop Jocelin preferred to overlook the latter sad years of his relationship with Becket, and probably also shared the king's remorse at the murder, and to recall his former close colleagueship with him, promoted a devotion to the new saint along with the dedication of many new churches in his honour. The dedication of an altar to St Thomas Becket in the cathedral at Sarum indicated the strength of the feeling there. This dedication was later transferred to the new cathedral, and within the liturgies of the Sarum Use there was provided a special procession on the saint's feast day, through a door in the north transept (now covered by a monument), to a cross of St Thomas which stood a few yards outside. The new city centre church was similarly dedicated.

It is worthy of note that one of Becket's senior staff members was John of Salisbury. He was the son of a Sarum canon, brought up as a chorister, acolyte and minor canon at (Old) Sarum, studying in Paris and eventually securing a post on the archbishop's staff. This connection with Canterbury might have seen an early infusion of Sarum customs to that cathedral except for the Benedictine Rule and customs already necessarily established there. John paved the way for the exiled Becket's return to Canterbury in 1170, and was a prime mover in the case for Becket's canonisation. John was then appointed to the post of canon treasurer of Exeter Cathedral, but his lack of residence there prevented another opportunity for the export of Sarum customs, though he did take his Sarum ideas and books to Chartres when appointed bishop there in 1176.

Jocelin remained at Sarum throughout Stephen's reign and that of the next king, Henry II, achieving for the cathedral and diocese a period of stability over forty-seven years. During this time he consolidated and promoted all aspects of the secular Sarum customs at a time of monastic revival. This latter was led by the Cistercians, an order formed largely by Stephen Harding, a novice monk from Sherborne.

The general relationship of Church and State began to improve from the year 1189 when Hubert Walter was appointed bishop, and Richard I came to the throne. Walter's capabilities were soon recognised and after only three years he was translated to be Archbishop of Canterbury. To his premier church post he added the top civil posts of chief justiciar and chancellor, the latter having been relinquished by Eustace, Dean of Sarum, on his translation to the bishopric of Ely. Whilst in this short time Hubert Walter would have effected little change at Sarum, his overall success and renown gave some reflection to his former cathedral.

Hubert Walter's successor, in 1194, was Herbert Poore, a local cleric from Dorset, whose father was Bishop of Winchester. He must have suffered increasingly bad experiences with the castle military authorities, along with other adverse conditions, as he began considerations for moving the cathedral away from the hill. Both the religious and civil communities' need for castle and rampart protection had waned and been replaced by a need for social stability and improved living conditions, not to say more space. His confidant in these discussions was his brother, Richard Poore, who was rector of St Martin's church, one of the bishop's manors a mile or so downstream where there was a ford crossing of the river on the main route south.

In 1197, Herbert appointed Richard to be Dean of Sarum, a move which was to facilitate the removal and rebuilding plan as well as the comprehensive re-writing of the customs and liturgical aspects of the Sarum Use. Progress was made on the latter, if not the former, when Richard was appointed Bishop of Chichester in 1215.

It was in this same year that another Sarum dignitary, and occupant of Sarum castle, made history of national importance. William Longspee, Earl of Salisbury, illegitimate son of Henry II and half-brother of the reigning King John, was a witness at Runnymede to the presentation of the Magna Carta, his name appearing in the early preamble to the document as *Willi comte Sar'* (William Count of Sar'um). This accounts for a sealed copy (all bishops and barons present at Runnymede would later have been supplied with one) being filed, first in the castle at Old Sarum, then in the library of the new cathedral, where Longspee was buried in 1225.

Richard Poore had been at Chichester only two years when his brother Herbert died in 1217. Richard was translated back as Bishop of Sarum, and may possibly have blamed the military's deplorable abuse of the clergy for his brother's death. He was determined to change the situation and the removal plans came out again.

4

TO NEW SARUM

Within two years of his return, Richard Poore had secured papal approval and royal support for the cathedral's resiting and rebuilding. His new site was one he knew well; an extensive meadow adjacent to the confluence of the Avon, Nadder and Wylye in his old parish of St Martin, already owned

Henry III depicted in the *Chronicle of England* by Peter Langtoff. The picture seems to indicate that the king gave bells (to be located in a separate bell tower) to the cathedral.

Extract from Richard Poore's Old Register (*Diocesan Record Office: WRO D1/1/1*). The second paragraph instructs on the alternating of sides of the quire for antiphonal singing. Line 1 ends '*ex pre decani alta ex pre cantoris*' – one side immediately following the other.

by the cathedral. According to Leland in the sixteenth century, the old Saxon church of St Martin stood near the ancient river ford (now Ayleswade bridge) where a busy hamlet had long since developed, probably in the St Nicholas area. It was said that the church was in a bad state of repair and river floods occasionally caused inconvenience such that it had to be rebuilt anyway. It could also be conjectured that so much of the church's land was needed for the expansive new cathedral, that it was more appropriate to rebuild the ruinous church elsewhere. It was, therefore, rebuilt onto another Saxon chapel half a mile northeast, the current St Martin's church.

The building of both St Martin's church and the cathedral commenced in 1220. The smaller church was built quickly and

The cathedral viewed from the north east.

consecrated by former rector, and bishop Richard Poore before his second translation to the bishopric of Durham in 1228. By this time also, the cathedral's three eastern chapels, following Roger's plan at Old Sarum, had been built and consecrated by Archbishop of Canterbury, Stephen Langton. The mortal remains of the illustrious former bishops at Old Sarum were translated to the new Trinity Chapel. (In other places this would have been the Lady Chapel, but the high altar, and thus the cathedral, was dedicated to the Assumption of the Blessed Virgin Mary, so a Lady Chapel, as such, was not required.)

It is a happy coincidence that the cleric-architect of the new cathedral plan was one Elias de Derham, formerly on the Canterbury staff of Hubert Walter and latterly Stephen Langton, and a close colleague of Earl Longspee in the effecting of the Magna Carta on behalf of the archbishop. Elias had been appointed to a prebendal canonry at Sarum and commissioned to supervise the grand plan for the building of a new cathedral and town. Canons' lodgings were built around the square of the Close, outside which was also begun the chequered plan of houses, inns and shops serviced by a grid of streets and river-fed drainage channels. The bishop, dean and chapter controlled

(Top) The reconstruction of Osmund's tomb in front of the Trinity Chapel altar.
(Above) A consecration cross carved and painted for the 1258 consecration (restored).

the whole comprehensive plan, realised, of course, on their own prebendal land. Thus it was that the bishop's judicial powers covered the civil city as well as the cathedral.

By 1258, in the episcopacy of Giles de Bridport, most of the cathedral plan had been achieved. It remained for the intricate west end to be completed, the cloisters, chapter house and, later, the tower and spire to be added, and for the city to expand further. On 30 September of that year, King Henry III attended the service of consecration. He was a generous benefactor, being also a close neighbour at Clarendon Palace which, concurrently, was being refurbished and extended. Again, Elias was supervising the work at Clarendon with Chilmark stone and Purbeck marble, the same materials as were being used for the cathedral. The building, at one and the same time, of a new cathedral, a new town and a royal palace, all within a couple of miles, must have constituted the most prestigious triple building project the country had ever seen. There is little wonder that Sarum became so widely known and respected, that many bishops came to the consecration, that many pilgrims visited, that many scholars sought a place here, and that constitutional and liturgical customs spread through the medium of these visits.

The 13th century saw the unique complex of New Sarum (still the official title of the city) well-established and flourishing, with a corresponding demise of Old Sarum. Much of the dressed stone from Old Sarum was brought down for building the Close wall; some 12th- if not 11th-century carvings can still be seen along Exeter Street. The eastern chapels in the old cathedral survived for some time and were used by a settlement of friars. It took centuries for the old town community to dwindle completely, and until the 19th century, as a 'rotten borough,' Old Sarum returned members of parliament.

Clarendon Palace gradually lost its favour as roving justiciars and rent collectors became phased out, and Tudor London blossomed into the chief centre for legal and financial government. At the same time, Normandy and France became of decreasing relevance, as did the New Forest hunting ground. The chief royal palaces were thus sited in the capital. Clarendon's final demise did not come until the end of the Tudor dynasty. Around 1662, the Lord Chancellor bought the estate and took from it the title of Earl of Clarendon. His family were involved in the printing business which then became known as the Clarendon Press, and is now part of Oxford University Press.

5

DOCUMENTS AND BOOKS

The last persecution of Roman Emperor Diocletian in 303 saw the systematic destruction of early Christian literature, and with it, all trace of early liturgy in the form of written prayers. In the middle of the fourth century, Serapion, a bishop in Egypt, wrote prayers for the eucharist, a collection of which was discovered in the Greek monastery of Mount Athos, and published in 1899. This was then translated into English by the scholar, former chaplain of Brasenose College, Oxford and Bishop of Sarum, John Wordsworth. In Serapion's prayer book we have access to, and understanding of the earliest Eucharistic prayer along with evidence of an invocation to change the elements 'that they may become the body of the Word … (and) the cup may become the blood of Truth…'

The first written forms of western use date from the fruitful period of the seventh century. Notable amongst these were the *Ordines Romani,* containing directions for the actual performance of each liturgical function.[11] Originally pertaining to the rites as performed in Rome itself, they were frequently copied and used as guides in many other centres. Mgr Andrieu identified fifty *ordines* or short chapters of instructions including: ten on the celebration of the mass by the Bishop of Rome; two on chants and lessons for the office of the hours; four on hours for prayers and meals; six on the ordination of priests and bishops; two on the consecration of churches and deposition of relics; one on rites for the dying, and three for the coronation of an emperor. The chapters on the Roman papal mass, particularly, give a good insight to the early Roman Use and its basis for developing western liturgical practice.

Pope Gregory's reputed modal classification of chants was specific in its directions as to reciting notes and finishing notes, but despite this, the verbal tradition required nothing written down. Chants were passed on through oral practice, and not until the ninth or tenth century was any satisfactory code for music invented. Only then were guidelines introduced to identify pitch movement in melodies.

After the innovations of one, then three lines for the stave, there settled the practice of the use of four lines. This grid

The seal of the church of Saint Mary, Sarisburiensis.

amply provided the modest range of notes to accommodate the known repertoire of chants, which, of course, developed naturally within the range of the average voice. Thus was born plainsong notation which was to be the literature of music for several hundred more years. Fortunately, some early manuscripts have survived the ravages of carelessness and wilful misuse to indicate this development.

Although Anglo-Saxon manuscript collections would undoubtedly have been taken by Bishop Herman from Sherborne to Sarum, nothing has survived the drastic audits and re-writings of subsequent years, other than a pontifical, the bishop's own book. Sherborne would have continued with its manuscript books geared to the Benedictine Rule, but its liturgy, and especially the supporting choreography and drama, is likely to have been that developed at Sherborne from its Celtic and Anglo-Saxon roots, with possibly a reverse influence by post-Conquest Sarum customs, at least whilst the Bishop of Sarum was still also Abbot of Sherborne.

One high profile document illustrating this is the *Sherborne Missal*. This is one of the finest English medieval illuminated manuscripts in existence, dated about 1400. It was compiled at the

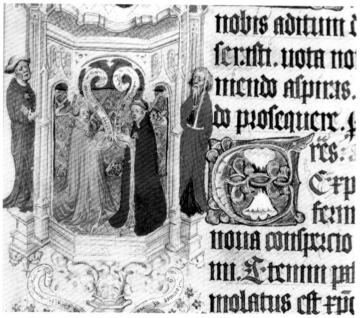

Sherborne Missal: detail from Easter Day. Bishop of Sarum with Abbot of Sherborne flanked by SS Peter and Paul (*Duke of Northumberland and the British Library*).

co-operative behest of both the Abbot of Sherborne and Bishop of Sarum, when the two posts were separated. Caricatures of the Abbot and Bishop are drawn in the margins of the manuscript. (The Missal belongs to the Duke of Northumberland and is housed at the British Library.)

Osmund's scriptorium at Old Sarum set about recording, first of all, copies of his new *Carta*, the essential reference for the constitution. As William the Conqueror had ordered the building of many huge, stone cathedrals, on a scale without Saxon precedent, there was a demand for this type of foundation document. The chief document to follow this was the *Institutio*. This laid down the developed hierarchical and prebendal organisation. The copy inherited by us today is now thought not to be Osmund's original. This *Osmund's Register*, currently in the County Record Office at Chippenham, is believed to be largely a century later than Osmund.

One of the first cathedrals to follow this constitutional *Institutio* was Wells, when the bishop's seat was moved from the monastic Bath Abbey back to the secular foundation in 1135. A few years later, Bishop Robert of Lincoln granted charters to his canons giving them the same liberties and immunities within their prebends 'as the canons of Sarum enjoy.'[12] Chichester also took the *Institutio* for guidance, and again, in 1214, it was quoted when the Lincoln chapter were advising the chapter in Moray, Scotland, on the organisation of a new foundation there.

The Consuetudinary was the book of ceremonial customs for the performance of the liturgy. The sources for the writings were, of course, the traditions of the time, themselves based on the earlier traditions of Sherborne and its ancient forefathers. After the foundation *Carta* and *Institutio* had run their initial and useful course, it was the liturgical customs of Sarum which became more in demand. Bishops and other clerical visitors, impressed by the literature, music and ceremonial at Sarum, desired to copy the same in their own establishments. Osmund's consuetudinary does not survive, but one developed during the following century, largely under Jocelin, does.

This latter was surely the basis for the more comprehensive consuetudinary of Richard Poore, written at the beginning of the 13th century, possibly whilst he was Dean of Sarum.[13] This contained eleven chapters on constitution, thirteen on general customs, and eighty on service details. Nowhere else was such depth of guidance laid down for a cathedral. Poore is credited as being the originator of the term 'Sarum Use.'[14]

In 1220, the distinguished gathering of bishops and clergy for the laying of foundation stones at New Sarum would have been impressed to learn first-hand of the Sarum service books. Within three years, the bishop of the Celtic foundation at St David's ordered that his cathedral's services for the Blessed Virgin Mary (Sarum's patron) were to be as in the *Ordinale Ecclesie Sarum*.[15] In 1226, a college of secular clergy at Merewell in the Winchester Diocese adopted the Sarum Ordinal, their own cathedral being monastic. Further evidence of instructions to follow the Sarum Ordinal has been found at Dublin, Moray, Glasgow, Elgin and Aberdeen. This indicates a recognisable Celtic element in the liturgy, originating, for Sarum, in the early days of the western kingdom's cathedral at Sherborne. In 1258, possibly after attending the magnificent ceremony of consecration at New Sarum, Bishop William of Glasgow conceded to his chapter, liberties and customs 'as the Church of Sarum.' In order to take the fullest possible advantage of this, the dean and chapter of Glasgow consulted directly with their colleagues at New Sarum on matters of detail, and in 1259 a newly written copy of the revised Consuetudinary was despatched to them.

The Lichfield Consuetudinary follows closely the earlier part of that at Sarum, whose later part concerning liturgy was not fully adopted but borrowed to some extent in the 13th century. The status and duties of the four principals does not entirely conform to the Sarum pattern. Exeter went its own very Celtic-influenced way, when it was founded on the transfer of the see from Crediton, at the time of Old Sarum's foundation. The chapter did not even have principals until the first dean was appointed in 1225, and this may have been due to the high-profile New Sarum foundation. The Exeter statutes from that date show similarities to those of Sarum. In 1327, Bishop Grandisson of Exeter sent to Sarum for a correct pontifical for his own use. He later produced an Ordinal including, for the first time, a record of Exeter customs. Much of this was derived from the Sarum Consuetudinary, although the duties of the four principals eventually elected, varied from those at Sarum.

In 1228, Pope Gregory IX had noted Sarum's esteem in liturgical expertise and at the same time as translating Bishop Richard Poore to the see of Durham, seems to have conferred a favour upon the appointment of bishop of Sarum, ex officio. A publication of 1608, *English Martyrology*, makes it clear: referring to 'ancient times' it records 'Bishops of Salisbury obtained the Title of the Pope's Maister of the Cerimonayes at Rome, according to that dignity.' [16] This was, presumably, an honour rather than a practical appointment, in the same way that other church honours were bestowed upon favoured clerics. In this respect, the bishop might have been described, unavoidably, as an 'absentee Master of Ceremonies.' An interesting point is that whilst there are papal bulls excommunicating Henry VIII, there is no record of the Bishop of Salisbury's title of Master of Ceremonies at Rome being relinquished! However, since the Reformation and superseding the above, the Bishop of Salisbury has traditionally been Provincial Precentor in the Archbishop of Canterbury's College of Bishops. Thus, at consecrations of bishops performed by the Archbishop of Canterbury, the Bishop of Sarum has the duty to commence the singing of *Veni Creator Spiritus* (now, commonly known as *Come Holy Ghost).*

A further boost to the spread of the use came in the 14th century when the consuetudinary was revised into a more general form, excluding some of Sarum's peculiarly local detail, and allowing the introduction of other, more widely useful material. This policy was particularly helpful to parish churches, whose buildings, architecture, robes and staffing resources were not on a cathedral scale, and where there was no observance of the lesser hours of Prime, Sext, Nones and Compline.

The demand for books came, of course, from bishops and priests responsible for performing the liturgy, not from congregations at large. The latter merely attended, particularly, the mass, and were not required to make any significant contribution or response. Secular cathedrals, priories of secular canons, such as Augustinian, and parish churches were the markets, and the latter included those churches in a diocese where the cathedral was monastic and duty-bound to follow the monastic rule. Thus, for instance, the many churches in the then highly populated diocese of Norwich followed the Sarum Use, and a Sarum breviary can be seen displayed at Ranworth church on the Norfolk Broads, believed to have belonged to a local Augustinian priory.

Ivychurch and Christchurch Priories would also have followed the Use.

Chief amongst service books was the missal. The mass had always been the central form of worship for Christians, and the missal collected all the standard prayers and directions for the performance of mass. The eleventh century Gallico-Roman missal of Rouen was a source of liturgy tapped by Osmund, which moulded with ancient Sherborne rites to shape what became the Sarum missal. The part of the missal content spoken or sung by the celebrant was usually contained in a sacramentary. Other missals for quire use often missed out much of the celebrant's material but included material for general participation. Copying was a laborious task and efficient thought was given to the particular use of any book produced.

A collection of books was required by quire clergy during mass: a processional for the litany and verses sung in the pre-mass procession; a gradual or grayle for the musical settings of the propers of the day; a *troper* for the additional lines of text added for decoration on special feasts; and a lectionary for the lesson readings, although a ceremonial text was used by the gospeller and epistoler. The hymnal eventually found a place in western liturgies, though its content varied considerably amongst uses.

The series of services of the hours, or the Divine Office, included Matins and Lauds (usually sung together, at midnight in monasteries, and often left until Prime in secular communities), Prime, at the first hour of daylight, Terce, theoretically at the third hour, Sext at the sixth, Nones at the ninth, then Evensong late afternoon, and Compline before retiring. These required another set of books: a pie or pica listing the order and general directions for services to be sung; an ordinal giving directions as to varying contents of services; a psalter for the words of the psalms; a *tonal* for the repertoire of tones or chants; and an antiphonal for the antiphons linked to the psalms and canticles according to festal observance.

The use of so many books was less than convenient and so there developed a breviary which was a briefing or condensing of all the daily offices and instructional rubrics in one book. One effect of this collation was a reduction in the length of lessons or scripture readings. What was formerly a chapter of scripture in the *legenda*, became contracted to a mere sentence or two in the breviary, though still referred to as a chapter (see the order of Compline currently in use). Similarly, later editions of the missal comprised also the gradual, the *troper* and all rubrics for directions throughout the mass. Rubrics were so called because they were written in red ink to distinguish them from the black text (Latin: *rubrica* = in red).

Other books of lesser use were the manual, for occasional services such as baptism, matrimony and burial; and the pontifical for the bishop's services of dedication, confirmation and ordination.

Over the years there were occasional revisions of the liturgy at Sarum (there was, of course, no central Liturgical Commission, nor any external guidance). Despite general accumulation of observances in the middle ages, some did become obsolete and were deleted. Other new prayers, hymns and sequences were added, and even new feasts added to the calendar. This was easy to effect with manuscripts before printed and bound books; one vellum page could be removed, and a new one inserted. Manuscripts were often beautifully illuminated by artistic clerics and scribes.[17] Whilst many were written in the cathedral library and cloisters, the demand for manuscripts, and later, books, was such that many scribes set up in business in the new city adjacent. Wealthy purchasers could commission highly illuminated copies, whilst less glamorous copies sold on the general market.

The medieval church strongly disapproved of incorrect or inconsistent ritual in its divine worship, and Sarum's regular updating of its liturgy contributed to its constant validity and appeal. It gained increasing value as an authoritative reference and source of proven customs and regulations for transplanting to other cathedrals, colleges and churches.

Sarum books also found their way onto the continent, especially to French territories held commonly under the Plantagenet kings. When the scholarly (Old) Sarum canon, John of Salisbury, was promoted to Bishop of Chartres, he took his Sarum books and transferred the Use to that cathedral, language not being a problem as all was in the common ecclesiastical Latin. Balancing the import of Mozarabic customs through pilgrimages to Santiago de Compostela, was the export of Sarum books to Portugal when Philippa of Lancaster, daughter of John of Gaunt, became the queen of John I of Portugal. Thus the Use was introduced at Braga in 1385.

In 1391, Sarum's new ordinal was obtained by Exeter, and Sarum customs were adopted there, except where they conflicted with established Exeter customs. The Bishop of Exeter, in 1505, required his chapter to conform fully with the ordinal and consuetudinary of Sarum. At Hereford, the early service books bore little liturgical relationship with those of Sarum, but a later manuscript ordinal, a printed breviary and a missal show some Sarum influence. York service books remained independent. London St Paul's was also independent in the early days, but at the end of the 13th-century and beginning of the 14th, the statutes were codified in a *registrum* for reference, and there is evidence there of borrowing from Sarum. This St Paul's document was also the basis for a *novum registrum* at Lincoln in the 15th century. At the same time, the Lincoln chapter consulted Sarum, following a dispute, regarding details of customs. This confirms both earlier borrowing from Sarum and the view that Sarum was the authoritative reference. St Paul's eventually adopted the Sarum Use completely in 1415 on the initiative of Bishop Richard Clifford, a former canon of Sarum.

Whenever a cathedral adopted the Sarum Use, this was deemed to be the diocesan form, and thus so followed its parish churches. Where cathedrals were monastic, their Benedictine rule was clearly unsuitable for secular church use, and the norm became for their parish churches to follow Sarum, as did many non-monastic priories of regular canons, chantries and collegiate institutions.[18] Colleges adopting the Sarum Use in the 15th century included Winchester, Eton, King's College Cambridge, All Souls and New College Oxford. Later colleges followed the same pattern.

This spread of interest and influence created an increasing need for service books, and the ability to produce them served the prospering cathedral and town of New Sarum very well. The general recognition of Sarum's lead in theological and liturgical scholarship attracted to the town many of those involved in the making of manuscript books; scribes, illuminators and binders, as well as students and scholars. The 13th-century town was sparklingly new and surely one of the most pleasant of towns in England in which to live and work. Many set up shops in the town and made a lucrative living from supplying clergy and churches, both inside and outside the town. The finest books, beautifully illustrated with bright colours and gold leaf, and beautifully bound in finest leather, were specially commissioned by the wealthy, which included many bishops, deans and prebendal clergy as well as secular land-owners and merchants. No other town or city in the country could boast so great and well-matched a demand and supply of handwritten liturgy.

In the second half of the 15th century, the development of mechanical printing favoured the most popular service books. Those of Sarum again obtained a distinct advantage as can be seen, for instance, in the relevant number of extant copies of 16th-century processionals: there have been recorded 62 of Sarum, and 9 of York. Of printed editions between 1475 and 1549, there were 51 Sarum missals against 5 of York; 42 Sarum breviaries against 5 of York; and 184 Sarum primers against 5 of York.[19]

England owes much to William Caxton, principally a printer of English language works, albeit a considerable amount of his work was done on the continent where the machinery was first developed. Naturally, the dominant Sarum Use books were a good source of revenue for him and were proliferated through many print runs. The best-selling of all printed books was not the bible but a Sarum primer. Caxton died in 1491, exactly 400 years after Osmund had handwritten the first generation documents in his scriptorium at Old Sarum.

6

EDUCATION

Education was provided for the boys of the new cathedral as previously at Old Sarum and Sherborne. This was largely geared to what was appropriate to their cathedral life: Latin, divinity, singing, reading scripture, and copy-writing. Most of the teaching was initially provided by the *archi-schola*, later to become the canon chancellor. A *magister scholarum* was a later and additional appointment. Liturgical music and singing was taught by the canon precentor.

The middle ages did not generally see schools outside cathedrals or monasteries. Paris was the nearest university until the 13th century and it was here that one or two of the wealthy Old Sarum canons were educated. In the early 13th century, a wealthy merchant's son from Abingdon, Edmund Rich, his popularly-allocated surname indicating his family's status, was taught at a church school adjacent to St Mary's, Oxford. After further education in Paris, Edmund returned to Oxford to teach in and develop the church school as a collegiate hall of higher education in theology and philosophy. Edmund became the most renowned teacher of his day and Oxford the nucleus of the first university in England.

One of Edmund's early students was the son of the wealthy Bishop of Winchester, Richard Poore. The two clearly formed a good relationship as in 1220, on the launch of the building of the new cathedral, Richard Poore, by then Bishop of Sarum, invited Edmund, by then an Augustinian friar and Oxford's prime theological preacher, to be New Sarum's first canon treasurer, taking charge of the new project, and no doubt bringing to it some promise of its development into a major educational institution. Edmund's success in his project and his growing personal renown, through his charm and charitableness, led to his appointment of Archbishop of Canterbury in 1233. He was viewed as a reforming bishop, showing both vision and diplomacy, but eventually the political difficulties of the time caused his exile to Pontigny where he died in 1240. He was canonised in 1247.

Easter Day Mass – part of an illustrated page from the missal of Sire Richard Sutton, (*Principal and Fellows of Brasenose College, Oxford*). Sir Richard, co-founder of the College, is depicted kneeling at the bottom under the words 'Of your charite pray for the sowle of Rychard Sutton ...'.

Education continued to be an integral part of the cathedral's mission. In 1261, Bishop Giles de Bridport established a College of St Nicholas de Vaux, adjacent to the St Nicholas hospital by the river bridge.[20] The canon chancellor supervised the college, and the normal establishment was up to seven priest-tutors or scholars, and some twenty clerks or students. Many scholars and students migrated from Oxford, partly due to New Sarum's appeal and partly to troubles and riots in Oxford. At one point it seemed that Sarum would take the collegiate lead in preference to Oxford. This accounts for the Oxford armorial shield's being displayed on the successor to one of the college buildings today. In 1270, Bishop Walter de la Wyle founded another college at the other end of the town, this in memory of the beloved St Edmund. This secular community comprised thirteen canons, and was endowed with fruitful property holdings.

By the end of the 13th century, Sarum was being described as a university town.[21] Its theological scholarship was second to none and, having three secular colleges, was equal to Oxford, if we count the cathedral which was indeed a secular collegiate house, and a major institutional advantage that Oxford did not have at that time.

Further confirmation of its being a prime educational centre was the settling in Sarum of the friars. The Dominican order, conscious of its special work to preserve catholic doctrine against heretical teaching, determined to establish foundations in every university town in Europe. They came first to the ancient shire capital and monastic town of Wilton, and then to Fisherton, a suburb of New Sarum. The Franciscans moved into the vacated cathedral at Old Sarum, and Carmelites into buildings east of the new cathedral.

The friars, themselves scholars, had a particular reputation for teaching and preaching. Whilst the secular clergy of the cathedral were adequately taught, they were more directly concerned with their official, liturgical, sacramental and pastoral duties, than preaching. They did not concern themselves extensively with the study or exposition of questions of a deep theological nature.

There seems little wonder that the Oxford cleric and scholar, Wyclif should write, in his treatise 'Of feigned contemplative life' in 1375:

> ...and so, if priests say their matins, mass and evensong after Salisbury Use, they themselves and other men deem it enough, though they neither preach nor teach the hests of God and the gospel. Ah Lord! If all the study and travail that men have now about Salisbury Use with multitude of new costly portos, antiphoners, grayles and all other books were turned into making of bibles .... [22]

The cathedral chapter took wide advantage of the preaching friars on those festal occasions when a sermon was merited, which was by no means every week. It was reported that throughout the year 1475 there were twenty sermons preached in the cathedral, nine of which were by the friars.[23] The rest would have been delivered by the bishop and dean, and maybe a principal canon but not by other clergy. Other canons would normally only preach in the parish churches of their prebends. The 15th-century *Novum Registrum* at Lincoln, influenced by Sarum customs, recognised sixteen sermon days as the four

Sundays in Advent, Christmas Day, Ash Wednesday and the ten Sundays from Septuagesima to Easter Day.

Even within the Church there were very widely different views as to what education should comprise.

7

QUIRE, NAVE AND SCREEN

As a secular cathedral, the Salisbury building was designed to accommodate both clergy and laity, in the quire and nave respectively, just as monastic institutions accommodated both clerical monks and lay brothers in a similar way. The clergy were the elite and therefore walled-off in their private quarters, as they had been since early Christian times, positioned in collegiate style to facilitate the *alternatim* or antiphonal practice of liturgical performance.

Each side of the quire (the word possibly derived from the quantity of two dozen in a collection, whether sheets of paper, monks, prebendal canons or other) was fitted with three rows of inward-facing seats allocated in true Norman feudal hierarchical form; the senior, prebendal canons in the back and upper, carved and titled stalls; the slightly lower, middle range of seats were for non-prebendal minor canons, and the front and lowest seats were for junior clergy such as deacons, sub-deacons, acolytes and lectors, and the (singing) boys.

The ancient Jewish priesthood was a forerunner of Christian clergy orders. Its hierarchy consisted of high priest, priest, and Levite (a lesser, assistant priest). The Byzantine Church still recognises five ordained orders; the major ones of bishop, priest and deacon, with lesser orders of sub-deacon, and lector or cantor. It also recognises non-ordained orders of candle-bearer and deaconess. Sarum and the English Church in general recognised seven orders; priest (including bishop), deacon, sub-deacon, acolyte, exorcist, lector and doorkeeper.[24]

Promotion was generally by age, or length of service. Singing-boys would graduate to lector or acolyte in their teens, and they could expect to be a sub-deacon at twenty, deacon at twenty-five, and priest at thirty. They might, nevertheless, through favour awarded to the family, be made a prebendal canon before being ordained priest. (Theodore in the 7th century and Thomas Becket in the 12th, to name but two, were appointed Archbishop of Canterbury before being ordained priest.)

In the early Church, bishops were elected from their particular local community to act as leaders. In later practice, the pope stepped in to effect some control and regularise appointments by his obligatory confirmation. In medieval England, William the Conqueror made sure of his control of England, partly through the Church, by appointing his own, Norman bishops. The pope was pushed into a secondary role of noting appointments, though by Plantagenet times, the pope regained increasing control.

Sarum's traditional appointment of prebendal canons was the prerogative of the bishop. On induction to their stalls, Sarum canons were invested with a book of canonical rules and a loaf, the latter representing the daily commons or share in the community's provisions, funded from certain, allocated income.[26] Priests were ordained through the bishop's laying-on of hands, as were deacons, these two ranks also being invested with chasuble and stole respectively. Sub-deacons and below were not ordained but appointed and admitted to their orders at a mass through the presentation of their instruments of office; a chalice for a sub-deacon, a candle-holder or wine cruet for an acolyte, a book of exorcism prayers for an exorcist, a book of scripture lessons for a lector, and the church keys for a doorkeeper.

It was not seemly that they should be observed in their liturgy by the laity, so even the division from the nave was a solid stone screen called the pulpitum. Against this screen were the seats of, on the more important right or south side but facing east, the dean, hence this became the decani side.[25] On the dean's right was the sub-dean, usually also archdeacon of Sarum. Across on the north side, also facing east was the precentor or first cantor, hence this became the cantoris side. The chancellor and treasurer took seats respectively south and north at the eastern corners of the quire. At the south-east corner also was the bishop's cathedra, convenient for the altar for when he was celebrating, preaching or blessing.

For most of the office, the clergy stood in their stalls facing across the quire, turning and bowing to the altar at the *Gloria Patri*, sung at the end of every psalm and canticle. Some respite from standing was enjoyed by the canons and minor canons by leaning on the up-turned seats which afforded a small, secondary seat at a higher level, and therefore, with some comfort, gave the impression of a constant standing posture. These beautifully carved seats were thus called misericords, their having mercy on the occupier. For much of the mass, all faced the altar which of course was the focus for most of the activity. Sitting was allowed to senior clergy during the epistle, gradual, alleluia or tract, but junior clergy and singing-boys on the lowest seats had to stand throughout.

In the early days, most of the fifty or so canons were resident and attended all services to sing the office or take an active part in the mass. The better singers undertook duties as *rectores chori* or rulers, which would now be called cantors, who rehearsed and led the singing after first taking the initial note or phrase from the precentor to ensure correct pitch. The normal practice was a ruler on each side, at a desk in front of the singing-boys, though two each side were prescribed for principal feasts. This duty of ruler was initially peculiar to Sarum, inherited from its Gallican and Celtic ancestry, although along with other aspects of the Sarum use, it was copied in other cathedrals. The organist and director of the choir of Southwell Minster still retains the title of Rector Chori. The special status of the rulers was indicated by their carrying silver wands of office. These were partly symbolic, but were useful indicators of when full chorus singing was to start. The present-day conductor's baton must be a descendant.

Vestments for the liturgy originate from the secular dress of the Roman Empire at the time of Christianity-promoter Constantine. In Mediterranean climes, vestments were thin and loose-fitting. The alb, a long, white tunic, alone seems to have developed for strictly religious purposes, its stark whiteness symbolic of purity. For the cooler climes of northern Europe, a more substantial garment was necessary. This cassock-type robe was made from sheepskin or fur pelts and called a *pellicium* (Latin: *pellis* = fur or hide). This was appropriate for general, non-liturgical wear, being warm and of dark colour, but for quire wear, and in order to conform to the white-albed Mediterranean practice, the Sarum canons developed a more loose white garment to fit over the *pellicium* (still needed for warmth), with a circular opening for over-head dressing, and almost full-length to cover most of the *pellicium* in the kneeling position. This was the *super-pellicium* which later corrupted to surplice. The surplice is therefore a truly Sarum garment. (The *cotta*, a shorter garment with square neck, albeit an ancient Roman servant's garment, was introduced to England by the re-instated Roman Catholic Church only in the 19th century.)

Around the head and shoulders, canons wore an almuce or cape with a hood, made from black cloth lined with black wool. The principal canons, under a privilege granted, it was said, by King

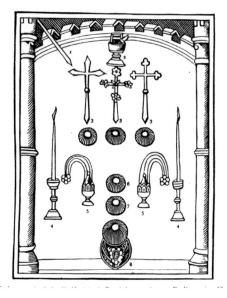

Ordo processionis in dei Nativitatis Domini ante missam. Ex
Processionalibus Sar. 1519-1558.

1 sacrista, virgam gestans.   2 puer, cum aqua benedicta.   3, 3, 3 tres
acoliti, cum crucibus.   4, 4 duo ceroferarii.   5, 5 duo thuribularii.
6 subdiaconus , textum deferens.   7 diaconus, textum deferens.   8
sacerdos, cum amictu, in capa serica.

Woodcut from a *Sarum Processional* showing the order for the pre-mass
procession on Christmas Day: Virger, boy with holy water, three crucifers (tonsured, as were all boys and clergy), two tapers, two thurifers,
subdeacon with epistles, deacon with gospels, celebrant with cope.

Edward I, were to wear almuces of grey fur lined with white
miniver fur, and black caps.[27] The sub-dean and succentor were
to wear almuces of plain calabre lined with white miniver.
Calabre was a reddish-brown wool from the sheep in Calabria,
southern Italy, which the Normans had colonised before England.
Miniver was the white fur of the Siberian squirrel. Over the
almuces, for much of the English year in an unheated cathedral,
all clergy wore a black wool cloak, full-length and close-fitting.
These were discarded in Eastertide when the white surplices
complemented the liturgical white of the season.

On double feasts, silk copes of the appropriate liturgical

colour were worn over the surplices by rulers and duty singers at the office and the mass. The dress for the altar party was full-length white alb, amice, which was a lightweight hood or collar of the feast colour, and girdle. Over these, with stole and maniple, the celebrant wore a chasuble, the deacon a dalmatic, the sub-deacon a tunicle, and acolytes tunics, all of the feast colour. These coloured vestments were often intricately embroidered and bejewelled, and more resplendent even than their original counterparts worn by the Roman magistrates and civic officials. The bishop's dress included a magnificent cope, mitre and gloves, the latter usually white and richly ornamented.[28] In cold weather he would also carry in his hand a small metal container holding hot charcoals, no doubt diverted from the thurible, to keep his hands warm.

The altar frontals were also most beautifully coloured and adorned. There was:

> one undying wish to make the house of God the throne of Christ, the altar more glorious than the houses of men, more dazzling with beauty than the thrones of earthly kings. The daughters and wives of kings, and the great ones of this world thought their leisure but too well filled up, and their wealth meetly bestowed when they themselves plied the needle in stringing their jewels on those sacerdotal garments they had worked from the correct and canonical, no less than beautiful, patterns which had been sketched for them by a Dunstan's (10th century) hand.[29]

One Anglo-Saxon princess, a great-niece of Edward the Confessor, expert in needlework, became Queen Margaret of Scotland, wife of King Malcolm. It is a fitting tribute to her that one of the current treasures of Sarum is the precious altar frontal in her chapel in the south transept.

For daily services there was no formal procession from a vestry to the stalls. Indeed, in the early days there was no vestry. Canons were always in their *pellicium*, and if necessary would bring their surplice from their home in the Close, moving directly to their stall in the quire. Mass vestments would be kept in cupboards in the quire aisle, the large chasubles and copes in the huge, wooden, semi-circular chests still occasionally seen in cathedrals.

West of the screen there were no seats or priorities of place for the laity, other than the general rule that men took the senior,

The medieval clock *c*.1360. It struck a bell to indicate time but had no face.

south side of the nave, and women the inferior north side. The ledges or stone benches on the wall sides were for the infirm to sit, giving rise to the expression for weakness or failure as 'going to the wall.'

The screen served another purpose in its pulpitum form. It was a platform, itself serving a double purpose. Firstly it was a focal stage on which the rood was displayed, that is the crucifix with adjacent figures of Mary and John, and this could be seen even from the west wall when the nave was full. Its second purpose was for the gospeller, to enable both clergy in the quire and laity in the nave to see and hear that highly important part of the mass, the gospel. To satisfy both sides, the gospeller faced north while singing the gospel to that most ancient of simple chants involving only three notes.

Because the screen effectively blocked the laic view of the high altar, some system was necessary to enable the laity to see some action of the mass, and especially the climactic consecration actions at the altar. For this purpose, a nave altar stood in front of the quire door, consecrated the altar of the Holy Rood, which of course stood high above. At this altar, a priest could see the high altar and would mimic the actions of the celebrant as a relay to the nave congregation. A sanctus bell would ring at the points of elevation as another indicator of the most holy point in the mass, when all must fall to their knees. As the actual consecration was at the high altar and not in the nave, the congregation would be administered unconsecrated bread, notwithstanding that the bread used for consecration at the high altar was provided by a lay family at the offertory. The family would present the loaves to an acolyte at the screen, who would take one only to the celebrant for consecrating.

In some smaller churches, there was often a squint allowing a view of the high altar from a transept chapel which enabled a secondary priest to perform similar actions at the chapel altar for the benefit of laity in the chapel. This indicated that in many churches, the screen, stone or wood, was an effective barrier. At Sarum, as at many other secular cathedrals, the screen also closed off the quire aisles. However, this meant that the main transept chapels were available to laity in the nave as and when masses were conducted at these chapels.

There was probably an hourly mass, announced by the hourly striking of the clock bell, at one or other of the altars in order to meet the demand from the constant stream of pilgrims, and as

Original pulpitum screen, with organ in 1754.

an altar was customarily limited to only one mass per day, several altars were needed. Thus, for pilgrim masses there were provided three chapels in each transept, as well as the central Holy Rood altar, and eventually additional altars between pillars down the nave.

In addition to this lay demand for daily masses, was the need of the priest clergy to celebrate mass regularly. The same single mass per altar rule applied and therefore a number of altars were required simply for clergy use. Hence, further eastern transept chapels were provided, as well as the three most eastern chapels, along with two other chantry chapels between the presbytery pillars.

It can be understood, then, in monastic churches where priest monks far outnumbered the lay brothers, and there was not normally a lay congregation, the screen was positioned further down the nave to allow the transept chapels for priestly use only. Such was the medieval division, whether secular or monastic, between clergy and laity.

The screen also probably housed the organ, both at Old and New Sarum, as one of its earliest functions was to accompany the processions, the routes for which extended from the west to the east ends. The early organ decorations on plainsong themes were called conductus because they were rhythmically helpful in leading the movement in the processions. No organ at Sarum is mentioned until 1463, when John Kegewyn was recorded as being the organist. In 1200 William de Wilton, organist, gave some land at Wilton for the benefit of the canons' communal fund.[30] It is likely that he came from a land-owning family in Wilton, the nearest significant residential area, and that he was a canon himself at Old Sarum, sharing in the same communal provisions. That there was no mention of organs earlier is probably because the instrument was secondary to the singing, and the organist was not the senior musician's appointment.

It is likely that both Old and New Sarum cathedrals had an organ immediately on their being built. Malmesbury Abbey in Wiltshire was noted for its organ in the 7th century when its founder, (Saint) Maildulf, himself built organs. His successor as abbot, (Saint) Aldhelm, was also a musician and refers in his writings to the gilding of organ cases. There can be little doubt that he would have initiated an organ installation at his 8th-century Sherborne Abbey, the seed-bed of Sarum's traditions. It seems unlikely that Sarum excluded itself from this musical history, and much more likely that, especially as a secular church, it was at the fore in the development of instrumental accompaniment.

Notwithstanding the secular lead in musical decoration, the 12th-century Winchester Abbey-Cathedral had a large organ of several stops or ranks of pipes, these initially at octave pitches to emphasise the melody being played. The four-inch wide keys would be played by hands rather than fingers, this being sufficient for melody only music. Two-part playing, which developed later in organum, required two organists at separate keyboards, and even three were known. The greater discipline for polyphonic accompaniment led to the natural development of smaller keys for one player to manage.

8

THE KALENDAR

The Sarum Kalendar, more recently spelled calendar, was adopted from the Anglo-Saxon calendar of Sherborne. It had 182 feasts on specific dates, with others of varying date from year to year. Of the latter was the major feast of Easter, fixed to the vernal equinox moon as the Hebrews observed the Passover, and as the Roman Use Gregorian calendar directed. Feasts linked to Easter were accordingly also variable.

Sarum's classification of feasts was different from other English uses, although in many respects there was concurrence. The main categories were doubles, simples and ordinary Sundays. The term 'double' refers to the greatest solemnity which required antiphons to be sung twice over. Whilst the normal, ferial practice was to sing only the first phrase of a psalm antiphon on its initial announcement, just to set the mode for the psalm, a double feast required the antiphon singing in full. Thus there was double the amount of antiphon singing.

Double feasts were sub-divided into principal doubles, greater doubles, lesser doubles and inferior doubles. Examples of feasts so classified are, respectively, Easter, All Saints, the Transfiguration and Saint Matthew. Simple feasts were classified as feasts of nine lessons or of three lessons. Matins of an ordinary day had one nocturn, which contained three lessons, and three responds. An important feast day Matins was accorded three nocturnes, and therefore nine lessons. An example of a simple feast of nine lessons would be Saint Osmund, whilst a feast of three lessons would be Saint John of Beverley, the former being of greater importance at Sarum, whilst the opposite would be true of the York use.

It was the Matins of nine lessons and responds which, re-visited in the 19th century in research on the Sarum Use, inspired Bishop Benson of Truro to emulate the format for a Christmas celebration, using carols instead of the plainsong responds. The origin of the Nine Lessons and Carols, is therefore traceable beyond the 20th-century tradition at King's College, Cambridge, and even the 19th-century at Truro Cathedral, to the medieval practice at Sarum.

Sundays were also classified as principal, greater, lesser or inferior, according to the feast, octave or season in which they fell. Non-feast days were ferial, and again classified as above, ranging from Eastertide weekdays to penitential Lenten weekdays. The rank of the feast determined not only the amount of antiphon singing but the whole complexity of the ceremonial including the number of vergers, crucifers, thurifers, acolytes, deacons and sub-deacons, and the number of rulers for the quire.

The Hereford Use, that form of Gallico-Roman use fostered in the west at Hereford Cathedral, had a less complex classification of feasts, as had the York Use and other secular uses. However, they had, quite naturally, feasts of local saints with higher recognition than that accorded at Sarum.

Sarum's liturgical practices and records did not remain static. The canons were noted for their being progressive in liturgical matters, and they took early recognition of the novelty in England of the feast of the Holy Trinity. Requests for higher recognition of the ancient doctrine of the Trinity were being made to Pope Alexander II in the mid-11th century, but he refused, saying that the Trinity was recognised daily if not hourly in the *Gloria* after every psalm and canticle. Notwithstanding the papal view, it was entered in the Sarum kalendar and the principal east chapel of the new cathedral was, in 1220, dedicated to the Most Holy Trinity (as the high altar, as at Old Sarum, was to be dedicated to the Blessed Virgin Mary).

John Peckham, Archbishop of Canterbury until 1292, wrote an office for Trinity, possibly copied from Sarum, and in the early 14th century, Pope John XXII ordered the feast to be observed by the whole church, on the Sunday after Pentecost. Where other uses continued the old Roman practice of numbering Sundays after Pentecost, Sarum innovated the sequence of Sundays after Trinity.

Likewise, there were demands for recognising a feast for Corpus Christi. In 1264, Pope Urban IV instituted the new feast, and a new liturgy was written by Thomas Aquinas. It was placed on the Thursday after the new feast of Trinity, to imitate the institution of the mass on the Thursday of Holy Week. Sarum took immediate recognition of the feast.

The Sarum kalendar's liturgical colours had roots in the ancient traditions of Sherborne, with new influences from Rouen, the Norman capital. The Sarum peculiarities, then, among English churches were: the exclusive use of white throughout Eastertide, and for feasts and octaves of the Blessed

Virgin Mary, even where these seasons included feasts of another colour; red for ordinary Sundays, including those after Trinity; green or blue for ferial days of Trinity and Epiphany; yellow for feasts of confessors; brown, grey or violet for Advent, Lent and other fasts and vigils.[31] The Lenten Sunday and Passiontide colour was red, as specified in the Gallican and Ambrosian uses, though the precise blood shade was said to have been taken from a Rouen Lenten processional cross.

Principal double feasts, being the great high days, were accorded the finest and most precious, jewel-encrusted vestments held by the cathedral, for which the precise colour was of secondary importance. This could possibly indicate that there was not so much mystery behind Sarum's liturgical colours as a practical necessity of using what vestments they had, and directions were simply framed around the inventory! Naturally, altar frontals, lectern and statue drapes also matched the vestments.

On Lenten ferial days, a fasting solemnity was observed by the use of dull, uncoloured, natural-shade vestments, with altar frontals and veils for images and crosses made from natural, undyed fabric, in what was known as the Lenten Array. This practice commenced on the first Sunday in Lent, whereas in other uses, veiling was restricted to Passiontide. A traditional feature promoted by Sarum was the Lenten Veil or the Great Veil, a large screen of natural silk fabric which was hung between the quire and altar to obscure and deny the luxury of sight of the altar and the elevation of the host. This was a relic from the early Christian practice whereby the altar was surrounded by curtains between four corner pillars supporting a canopy from which was suspended a pyx containing the reserved sacrament.[32] This in turn was derived from the veiled Holy of Holies in the Jerusalem Temple. The most holy focal point was not to be seen too readily. The windlass used for windingup the veil can still be seen on a pillar in the north presbytery. It was dramatically caused to fall at the words of the Passion gospel in Holy week, 'the veil of the Temple was rent in twain.'

There was much in the way of special observances in Holy Week. Matins and Lauds on the last three days of Holy Week assumed the name Tenebrae as a special, triangular frame holding 24 candles, a tenebrae or Lenten hearse, was erected before the altar. One candle was extinguished at the beginning of each antiphon and each lesson respond. With three nocturns

The windlass handle used to wind up the Lenten Veil or the Great Veil, which was hung between the quire and altar to obscure and deny the luxury of sight of the altar and the elevation of the host. The handle can be seen on a pillar in the north presbytery.

of Matins, there were nine antiphons and nine lesson responds, and with a further six antiphons for Lauds, all candles were thus extinguished leaving a symbolic darkness.

On Maundy Thursday, following the main mass, at which the bishop traditionally celebrated, with seven deacons and seven

Worshippers outside the western door of the cathedral celebrating the Easter Vigil (*Salisbury Newspapers Ltd*).

sub-deacons, was the stripping and washing of the altars. Each of the many stone altars was cleared of its frontal, cloths and adornment, and washed with wine and water. This was followed by a gathering of the chapter in the chapter house for the washing of feet, and the agape, the sharing of the loving-cup.

The liturgy for Good Friday included the singing of the

Reproaches and the Creeping to the Cross, all remnants from the flamboyant Gallican Use. Holy Saturday's Easter Vigil rite began with new light freshly taken from the fire of palms to light the huge Paschal Candle which bore large grains of incense to represent the five wounds of Christ. During the candle's procession, the deacon sang the great and ancient Easter hymn of praise, the *Exultet*. It may have been written as early as the 5th century but its first appearance was in the 7th-century Gallican Bobbio Missal, and only later was it copied into the Roman Use, possibly by Alcuin under Charlemagne who wished to resolve all uses into one Roman Use. Its Gallican origin almost ensured its transfer through the Celtic contacts to the west of England's Sherborne traditions.

When positioned on its high stand, the Paschal Candle rose to some thirty-six feet in height. This was not only to give it a high prominence during Eastertide liturgies, but to enable people down the nave to see it over the quire screen. The tentative participation of the laity was merely by seeing the objects of holiness, few though such opportunities were.

Eastertide observances also included the building of an Easter Garden. On a tomb-top in the north presbytery, a model garden was built and on Good Friday the reserved sacrament was placed in the tomb to indicate the true presence of Christ there. It was taken out during the Easter morning ceremonies to indicate the Resurrection. This, of course, was for the benefit of the quire community only, though it is likely that another garden, without sacrament, was placed in the nave for general adoration purposes.

9

THE PROCESSIONS

Every Sunday before the principal mass, and similarly on all
double feasts, there was a procession round the cathedral
during which was sung a Litany, a sequence of petitions and
responses. The Litany was an integral part of the Eucharist in
the early Byzantine rite. Saint Chrysostom, in 398, introduced
processions with responsorial singing through the streets of
Constantinople, the new Latin city on the site of the Greek
Byzantium, and with petitions particularly for the common
needs of daily life and freedom from famine and plague. In 477,
Mamertus, Archbishop of Vienne in Gaul, ordered litanies to
be sung for three days before Ascension Day because there had
been a disastrous earthquake in the Rhône valley.

These days are still observed and known as Rogation Days
(Latin: *rogare* = to pray), although their purpose expanded to
embrace a more positive aspect of the land in a pagan Spring
procession of prayer for the fruits of the earth. This outdoor
procession of agricultural petitions was the basis of the Rogation
procession round the town of Old Sarum, and later, New
Sarum, which included a celebratory service in one of the town
churches, and of course the cathedral's internal processional
Litany before the mass.

All clergy and juniors, having entered the quire randomly as
usual, were in their places, and the people in the nave, when the
solemnities began. Water and salt were brought to the high altar
to be blessed and mixed to form the holy water for sprinkling as
a purification and absolution during which was sung *Asperges me*
from Psalm 51, calling for a purging and doing-away of offences.
The celebrant first sprinkled the high altar of the Assumption
of the Blessed Virgin Mary, which, in the 15th century stood
one bay forward from its present position.[33] He then sprinkled
the deacon and sub-deacon before proclaiming a versicle with
response and a collect. The procession then commenced, all
being sprinkled as they passed the celebrant or the celebrant
passed them. The verger, possibly two, robed with surplice,
led the procession to clear a way through the people in the
nave, who, without pews or chairs, stood randomly in groups.

The high altar. Today this is located one bay east of its original position.

Following the verger(s) were the crucifer(s) and acolytes with tapers, thurifer(s) and incense boat-boy, sub-deacon(s), deacon(s), celebrant, singing-boys and clerks of the lowest order, minor canons of the middle order, and prebendal canons of the highest order, principal dignitaries, and the bishop.

The normal processional route at New Sarum led from the presbytery step through the north quire door into the north quire aisle, clockwise round the east end, down the south quire aisle and, in summer, round the cloister, or down the south nave aisle, round the west-end font and up the centre of the nave. All chapel altars were sprinkled as the celebrant passed nearby, and a station was made before the St Cross altar before the rood screen. At this point, the celebrant turned to the people and, in the only vernacular of the service, read the bidding prayer, another Sarum peculiarity. This included a list of all who were to be prayed for in the mass, resorting to the normal Latin again for the Pater noster, versicles and Psalms 67 and 130. The procession then continued into the quire where seats were re-taken for the singing of the office of Terce. During Terce, the altar party went out to the canons' cemetery east of the cloister to sprinkle the graves, after which they returned to robe for the mass.

On principal double feasts, ironically, there was a shorter procession which led from the quire west through the rood

Statio ad fontes hebdomada Paschae. Ex processionalibus Sar. 1502, 1508, 1530 Rehnault.
1 cruciferarius. 2,2 ceroferarii duo. 3 thuribularius. 4,5 oleum et crisma. 6,6 rectores duo secundarii. 7,7,7, tres pueri cantantes '*Alleluya*' 8. puer ferens librum. 9,9 rectores chori principales. 10 executor officii. 11 fontes.

West wall quatrefoils (interior) through which the boys sang on Palm Sunday.

screen, through the south transept to the cloister, round the font and up the nave. This shorter route was to compensate for the extended mass which was to follow on principal double feasts, and accordingly the sprinkling of altars and canons' graves was omitted, as was the bidding station.

On each day in the octave of Easter, a short procession was made after Evensong. This was from the quire to the font only, where additional psalms were sung and baptismal vows renewed. The font was censed, and a collect sung before the procession returned up the nave. A station was made at the rood altar which was also censed, versicles and responses and a collect sung. A final psalm was sung to conduct the clergy once more into the quire.

The most elaborate and eloquent of all processions was, as with Jesus himself entering Jerusalem, that of Palm Sunday.[34] This representation was first enacted in the 4th century in a procession from the Mount of Olives into Jerusalem, copied in the 5th century in Mozarabic Spain, and in the 7th century in the Gallican Use. Aldhelm mentions in 709 a special singing of *Hosanna*. It thus appears in a root of the Sarum Use before it was adopted by Rome in the 12th century. It was in fact a double procession, one internal and one external. The external one led out into the town where all would stare and wonder, and fall to their knees, not just at the donkey and staged Christ figure,

West wall quatrefoils (exterior) behind the statues.

with waving palms, but at the most holy, consecrated Host in the monstrance held high by a priest. As this procession led back to the cathedral, with following crowd, it met, outside the west end, the internal procession coming from the cloister. At this point, the singing-boys, positioned internally up in the west gallery, sang through the quatrefoil openings the festal antiphon *Pueri Hebraeorum*, which ends in *Hosanna*, though after the birth of music notation and the development of complexity in plainsong, possibly not exactly the *Hosanna* which Aldhelm recorded.

10

THE MASS

The mass has always been central to Christian worship, originating as it does from the Lord's Last Supper, and the equating of the elements of the supper with the Lord's body and blood. The solemnity with which it was thought appropriate to conduct the mass demanded abundant, precise and consistent ceremonial. Flamboyant would be the term for explaining that ceremonial which developed in the Gallican and Mozarabic traditions, these, in turn, being the seedbed for the western Anglo-Saxon traditions.

The origins of many aspects of the mass ceremonial in fact go back further than the Last Supper, to the ancient ceremonial of the Temple, and to the classic drama of the Greeks, much revered in Roman times. From these sources were derived altars, candles, incense, high priests, assistant priests, coloured vestments, singing of the law and the psalms, and the modal organisation of music and chants.

By the 4th century, the Syrian Church had established a Eucharistic pattern of two lessons, reminiscent of the law and prophets readings of Judaism, read from a pulpit, a sung psalm, and a gospel reading, for which all stood.[35] An address was given by a senior priest and also, if he be present, by the bishop who sat in the Roman-style semi-circular apse of the basilica facing the people across the altar. The bishop's deacon led a litany of petitions to which the people responded. The greeting by the *kiss of peace* was exchanged and the elements for the eucharist were brought up by lay representatives. The long Eucharistic prayer followed, terminating in a joyful respond from the people which included hymns we would now recognise in the *Gloria in excelsis*, *Sanctus*, and *Benedictus*. Communion in both kinds was administered to all present before a blessing from the bishop and dismissal by the deacon.

After the Council of Nicaea in 325, the newly-formulated *Credo* was introduced to the Byzantine Church. It took another two centuries for it to appear in the Spanish Mozarabic Use, and not until the 11th century was it integrated into the more rigid Roman Use, probably at Cluny, and then into the monastic tradition of Sherborne. There was a practical reason for its introduction which will be discussed later.

Many instances of early ritual accompanied the spread of Christianity itself. These were influenced by local traditions and observances, often promoted for the recognition of local saints, with accompanying literary accretions to the liturgy. By the 11th century, many western cathedrals rejoiced in their own peculiarities within a Roman Use framework. Sarum, of course, inherited much that was flamboyant, and ritual in some measure was employed for all worship, including robing procedures, and ample burning of incense at both Matins and Evensong. Ritual was at its most elaborate in the principal mass (High Mass was a term introduced only in the 19th century).

Whilst the quire clergy continued with Terce, the altar party robed into their mass vestments in the south quire aisle. The very audible Terce office hymn *Veni Creator Spiritus* was therefore necessarily the preparation hymn for the celebrant and assistants. This arrangement was, initially, peculiar to Sarum, though later copied into the Bangor Use.

If the celebrant was one of the chapter, he would have one deacon and one sub-deacon; if the bishop, on a Sunday or Simple feast, he would have three deacons and three sub-deacons; on a Double feast, he would have five of each; and for his usual celebrations on Maundy Thursday and Pentecost, seven of each.

The mass commenced with what we know as the *Introit*, though at Sarum, uniquely in England, it was known as the *Officium*. This term was also used in the Mozarabic Use at Santiago de Compostela, which would indicate the early western connection with the Celtic-based traditions, as well as the pilgrim traffic between Sarum and Compostela. During the singing, the party, here led by thurifer(s) as vergers were not required to clear a way in the presbytery, made their way through the south quire door to the altar.

The *Officium* or *Introit* was a biblical verse, proper for the day, with antiphon, psalm verse and *Gloria Patri*, with certain repeats depending on the rank of the day. It is believed to have been first introduced as entrance cover by Pope Celestine I in about 430. The singing was started by the rulers for the day after a note pitched by the precentor. They sang the first phrase, and the rest of the quire joined in at a point indicated by the rulers. The musical settings for these 'propers' were collected in a gradual or grayle.

During the singing in the quire, the celebrant and assistants began their confession and preparation before the altar. After the *Officium* came the *Kyrie*, during which the celebrant censed the altar, the deacon censed the celebrant, and the thurifer censed the other clergy. The *Kyrie* is still in its original Greek of the early Church, but with such limited words and frequent repetition in litanies, its original form endured into Latin liturgies, initiated by Pope Gelasius in about 495. Pope Gregory records that on ferial days the long petitions were to be omitted and only the responses (*Kyries*) used. By the 8th century this chorus-only became standard practice, except in the Mozarabic Use where, surprisingly, the *Kyrie* was not specified at all. It was the Gallican Use which established the format of three *Kyries*, three *Christes*, and three further *Kyries*.[36] At Sarum, these were sung in full by the quire clergy, after the precentor's note and rulers' start as usual.

In time, because it was so simple, it became embellished with additional phrases called tropes (Greek: *tropoloyea* = modification) which were intended to highlight certain texts to add more glory to the feast. For instance, the *Kyrie* '*Orbis factor, Rex immense eleison*' began not only 'Lord have mercy' but 'Maker of the world, King eternal, have mercy.' These troped texts thus became related and peculiar to certain feasts. For the feasts of Epiphany, Pentecost and Corpus Christi there was sung not simply '*Kyrie eleison*,' but '*Kyrie, fons bonitatis ...*' or 'Lord, fountain of goodness, Father unbegotten, from whom all good things do come, have mercy; Lord, who bestowest seven-fold gifts by the Spirit with which heaven and earth are fulfilled, have mercy' etc. The succeeding Christe and *Kyrie* verses were similarly troped.

Troping became fashionable in the 13th and 14th centuries as a natural literary and musical development, still lateral rather than vertically harmonic. The framework of the ordinary being set, it was a simple matter for locally-composed inserts to be added. Thus, many ordinaries took on a distinctive style belying their basic description and becoming specific ordinaries restricted to certain days or seasons. The Sarum collection, troped and untroped, eventually numbered twenty-four, whilst Hereford had sixteen, some of them common to Sarum, but York had no York-specific, plainsong *Kyries*.

The *Kyrie* was followed by the *Gloria in excelsis Deo*, except, in accordance with the Mozarabic Use, during the penitential seasons of Advent and Lent. The *Gloria* was first used in the night office of the eastern Church, at the hour when St Luke's gospel records the visitation of the shepherds and the singing of the

Celebrant, deacon, sub-deacon and acolytes in a Sarum Bow at a present-day Eucharist.

angels.[37] In the 4th-century western use, it found a place in the night office of Lauds, and by the 5th century it had transferred into the mass because of its frequent midnight celebrations directly adjacent to Lauds.

The celebrant intoned the opening phrase of the *Gloria* standing centrally before the altar, to which also all in the quire turned. The quire clergy then turned back to face across the quire, in their normal misericord position, to sing the *Gloria* verses antiphonally. However, all turned again to the altar and bowed (such was the Sarum reverence; genuflection was never used at Sarum) at the words (translated) 'we worship thee,' 'receive our prayer,' and from 'thou only O Christ' to the end, there making the sign of the Cross.

There were nine settings of the *Gloria*, the ninth only being troped for use on feasts of the Blessed Virgin Mary, Sarum's patron. All remained facing the altar for the rest of the mass except at the epistle, for which clergy sat, the gospel, for which all faced the deacon-gospeller on the pulpitum, and the offertory.

After the *Gloria* came the prayers for special needs and collects which collected all the petitions relevant to the people and the feast. Such summarising prayers were probably introduced by

Pope Leo around 450, and were identifiably Roman in their consistent format and efficiency of wording. The Roman Use employed only one collect where other western uses included several. At Sarum there were commonly three, but up to seven were allowed, reflecting the seven petitions in the Lord's Prayer. The rule became established for an odd number of collects, and if an even number resulted from normal selection, then the collect for All Saints was added to make the number uneven.

Readings of scripture were reduced from three to two in most uses by the 7th century. By this time also there were authoritative lectionaries directing specific readings for feasts and seasons. The first of the readings at the mass, unlike that in the office, was usually from the epistles of St Paul, these being the earliest of New Testament writings. At Sarum, the epistle was sung by the sub-deacon from the pulpitum on Sundays and feasts, thus being seen and heard by laity in the nave. On ferial weekdays there wasn't this same demand so the epistle was then sung from the quire step.

Musically, the reciting inflexions for the epistle ranged from one note above to two notes below the reciting note. At the end of the epistle, two boys in surplices, bowing to the altar, moved to the pulpitum to intone, after a note from the precentor, the Gradual sentence, which, like the *Officium*, was a proper for the day. If the day was a double feast, three clerics in silken copes replaced the two boys. The whole quire joined in the Gradual after the intonation. On a double feast, it was repeated, thus distinguishing the feast with a double performance.

The *Alleluya* is another word which, being short and often used, has been retained in its original language form. It was first used in the 5th-century Roman Use as an extra solemnity for Easter Day. By the 6th century it had extended throughout Eastertide of several weeks, and was in general use by the 7th century. It does not appear in the Gallican Use, and in the Mozarabic it appeared after the gospel. At Sarum it was placed after the Gradual, except in Lent when it was omitted. The boys or clerics sang the first *Alleluya* and the proper verse, the quire repeating the *Alleluya* at the beginning and the end. The final syllable of *Alleluya* in western uses before Sarum, eventually settled into a neum, or compound note, of up to a hundred notes in a seemingly endless flourish of a coda. This practice developed from a vocalised improvisation on the final syllable to cover the deacon's procession until he reached the station for the gospel so there was no hiatus of silence.

By the time of Sarum's early days, whilst many *Alleluyas* were still protracted to a final neum of up to forty notes, many of the vocalised sequences had been separated and injected with words, often reflecting the message of the epistle just delivered. In later compositions, these became structured metrical verses or prose called a Sequence. The composition style was often simply one note to a syllable. The first verse was begun by the rulers and continued by the duty side of the quire. Subsequent verses were then sung by alternate sides until the last verse when all sang in full.

Sequences were sung on certain Sundays and double feasts but not in Lent. Replacing the festal *Alleluya* and Sequence in Lent was the Tract, which usually comprised several verses from the penitential psalms, sung by four canons or senior clerics in Lenten-red copes, standing at the quire step.

During the *Alleluya*, Sequence or Tract, the vessels were prepared on the altar. The altar was censed again and after the deacon's blessing, the gospel procession moved to the pulpitum involving thurifer, acolytes with tapers, sub-deacon and deacon. The deacon sang the gospel in similar musical manner to the epistle except that the inflexions did not include the note above the reciting note. This very simple chant is probably the oldest currently in use and clearly goes back to the Jewish scripture recitations in the synagogue, the reciting note taking most of the recitation, whilst the note lower was employed for the words of the Lord.

For the gospel, the deacon faced north so as not to have his back either to the celebrant at the altar or to the laity in the nave. Clergy in the quire bowed first to the altar then turned to face the gospeller. An early practice on completion of the gospel was the handing of the sacred text around the quire for all to kiss in solemn acknowledgement and dedication. An inventory of 1222 describes a text of gospels bound in solid gold, ornamented with 20 sapphires, 6 emeralds, 8 topazes, 8 almandine stones, 8 garnets and 12 pearls.

This gospel-kissing by a full quire took so long that some covering chant was thought desirable. This may have been the origin of the introduction of the *Credo*, though at Sarum it was only sung on Sundays and feast days. Thus, whilst the text was passed round, the celebrant moved to the centre of the altar to intone *Credo in unum Deum*, the quire continuing in full to the end. Although the Roman Use adopted the *Credo* soon after the adoption of musical notation, and there soon developed four compositions, Sarum's partial use of the *Credo* required only the one setting, which then became the common English setting, to be seen in the Appendix, commencing, as the quire needed *Patrem omnipotentem*. A bow (*inclinatus*) was made at the beginning of *Credo*, at the words (translated) 'and was incarnate …,' at the words 'and was crucified …' and at the concluding 'life of the world to come.' All faced the altar, and did so until the end of the mass except for the singing of the Offertory.

The Offertory was the offering of the oblations of bread and wine at the altar. Representatives of the town people in the nave, by rota, traditionally brought the elements to the nave, St Cross altar. There they were used for distributing to the laity, unconsecrated, whilst at the high altar, the celebrant used the unleavened bread called, at Sarum, the *sacrificium*. It also became so known at Bangor, though Hereford referred to it as the *panem*, and the Roman and York uses as the *hostiam*.

The chalice, with wine and water, and the paten with sacrifice, were lifted up by the celebrant as he said an Offertory prayer. The oblations were then censed prior to the censing of all in the quire, individually no less, by the thurifer, followed by the sub-deacon's presentation of a text of scriptures again, which each kissed following his censing. If the bishop was celebrating, there were two thurifers and two sub-deacons with texts. During this activity, there was sung the Offertory proper, which was conveniently long enough to cover most of the action.

On completion of the Offerory, the celebrant symbolically washed his hands in holy water at the greater, south side of the altar. It was therefore normal at such places adjacent to the altar, for the siting of a piscina or stone basin which allowed used holy water to run decently to ground, as was strictly required, that is, it must not be put down any man-made drain. Where there were two chapels sited adjacently with no separating wall, then a double piscina was built in the nearest south wall. Such can be seen at St Stephen's altar at the head of the south quire aisle, at St Nicholas's altar at the south-east transept, now a vestry, at St Michael's altar in the south transept, and at similar points in the north transepts.

With the Offertory concluded, the secrets were said. These were semi-audible prayers spoken by the celebrant but not generally audible beyond the altar. The number of such prayers was made to match the number of collects used earlier in the mass. The unity of worship was regained in the proclamation of the *Sursum corda* and its response, which led to the Preface, including perhaps one of the ten proper Prefaces according to the feast.

The solemn mood was set for the canon of the mass by the singing of the *Sanctus*. The rulers intoned the first word in the usual way, then all sang it in full, still facing the altar. Sarum had ten settings of it, which, of course, included *Benedictus* as an integral part, the precise setting chosen depending on the rank of the day. There was minimal troping to this ordinary and then only on feasts of the Blessed Virgin Mary.

All were then to kneel, except in Eastertide. The celebrant recited the canon with due ceremonial, followed by several prayers; one for the restitution of the Holy Land to Christianity, clearly dating from the Jerusalem Crusades of the 12th and 13th centuries; one for the king, and one for the bishop. Holding overhead the sacrifice and chalice, the celebrant then recited the versicle for The Peace, to which the people replied. If the bishop was present, there was also at this point the one and only blessing.

The *Agnus Dei* followed immediately. It was thought to have been imported from the east to the Roman Use in about 700 to cover the fraction or breaking of bread at the end of the prayer of consecration. The chant was begun by the rulers and continued in full throughout. There were ten settings in the Sarum repertoire, not normally troped.

After the *Agnus Dei* there followed the actual passing of the Kiss of Peace. It was a greeting often mentioned in St Paul's writings. It was not a general free-for-all greeting, but organised to pass down in a formal manner from the altar to the worshipping people. The celebrant initiated the greeting to the deacon who then greeted the sub-deacon who in turn passed it to the quire rulers who passed it to their respective sides of the quire; the canons of the higher form first, then the middle form of minor canons and deacons, then the lowest form of sub-deacons and acolytes. In the Byzantine, Mozarabic and Gallican uses, the Kiss of Peace followed the singing of the Offertory. In the Roman Use it came much later, following the post-consecration Lord's Prayer. Only in the Sarum Use did it, appropriately, follow the plea of the *Agnus Dei*: '*dona nobis pacem*' (grant us peace).

At the principal mass only the celebrant partook of the elements, the clergy having communicated earlier at a low mass. The ablutions then followed immediately, and during this short time the Communion proper was sung, this being a short verse commenced by the rulers and completed by the quire.

Then followed the post-communion prayers, the celebrant singing them in similar manner and number as the collects and secrets of the day.

Finally, the deacon sang the dismissal '*Ite missa est*' (the mass is ended) if the *Gloria* had been sung previously, or '*Benedicamus Domino*' (Let us bless the Lord) if not, to one of the fourteen chants which matched the *Kyrie* chant of the day. All responded '*Deo gratias*' (Thanks be to God).

There was no final blessing, and the altar party, after bowing to the altar in unison, departed, the celebrant quietly reciting the first fourteen verses of St John's gospel. On disrobing in the quire aisle, there were further prayers, versicles and responses. Meanwhile, the office of Sext had immediately commenced in the quire. One and a half, or two hours of mass, even without a sermon, earned no respite from the daily round of the Divine Office which continued relentlessly.

11

THE DIVINE OFFICE

The Divine Office had no sacramental element but consisted of psalms, prayers and bible-readings according to the traditional plan. Its origins were in the Jewish synagogue worship, but morning and evening prayers had long been common to Jewish families in their homes. Monastic practice of the 4th century was based on this routine.

The Jewish Temple also held three services of sacrifice throughout the day, at the third, sixth, and ninth hours in Roman chronology. It was at the latter, the hour of the evening sacrifice, when observance of the following day's festivities were anticipated. Thus the ninth hour, or 3 o'clock in the afternoon in modern chronology, was the earliest time at which a feast could be observed, and this became the basis of medieval Christianity's First Vespers or First Evensong of the feast the day after.

By the 6th century, the Roman Church had opted for a daily routine of seven services through a literal interpretation, and therefore a misinterpretation of the symbolism, of the psalmist's 'seven times a day do I praise thee O Lord.' The Hebrew psalmist, of course, used the ancient and significant meaning of seven as 'all the time' not a specific number. Right from the beginning, then, the seven 'hours' of the office were based on a false premise, the reason being that by the 4th century, there were no Jews in Christianity to give accurate interpretation of the relevant psalm. This accident, nevertheless, promoted the practice which was taken up by all monastic institutions. Secular cathedral communities, like Sarum, also favoured the format. It was a useful discipline and rule of life for the canons as well as a central and perpetual source of worship for, and on behalf of, the wider diocesan community.

The daily pattern of the office commenced with Matins, being, as its name indicates, the morning office. In monastic churches, it was placed after midnight, though in secular churches with a less vigorous regime, it's delay was often allowed until it could merge with Prime at dawn. Usually incorporated onto Matins was Lauds, so called because its allocated psalms were the *Laudate* psalms, the last four of the 150.

The Psalter was sung through completely every week and

Matins and Evensong, being the principal offices, took the large share of the daily rotation. The canticle at Matins was originally *Gloria in excelsis*, and this was replaced by *Te Deum laudamus*. Because this was not a Hebrew psalm but a text of Latin prose, psalm tones fitted awkwardly and special chants were devised for it. Further solemnity was afforded by incense as the altar and clergy were censed. The canticle at Lauds, *Benedictus*, was also regarded as solemn, and employed the solemn version of the chants, that is with the initial intonation used for every verse. Its antiphons too were generally more elaborate and sung in full at beginning and end.

Prime was sung, as its name implies, at the first hour of daylight. It was regarded as a minor office, along with Terce, Sext, and Nones, and with the other minor offices took a share of Psalm 119 to ensure its complete recitation over the week: three psalms, antiphons, lessons and responds in each nocturn. Double feasts and simples of nine lessons were accorded three nocturnes, and in this case, the first two nocturns' six lessons were, as normal, scriptural, the lectors in normal surplices, whereas the last nocturn employed non-scriptural material, often from a homily based on the life of the saint being commemorated, the lectors robed in silken copes to honour the feast.

Terce came at the third hour, though probably nearer the fourth hour on Sundays as it immediately preceded the mass. Sext was at the sixth hour, around midday, and on Sundays, after the mass. Nones was at the ninth hour, in the afternoon.

Evensong is an Anglo-Saxon name and was always used in the Anglo-Saxon diocese of Sherborne, descending then to Sarum. Throughout the Middle Ages it was unique to Sarum as all other churches, monastic and secular, used the Roman term of Vespers. This office came in the late afternoon or early evening when the candles were lit, following its origin in the Jewish tradition. Its main purpose was the singing of a large portion of the psalms on a daily rota of the weekly cycle. The solemn canticle of *Magnificat* was duly recognised with a full recitation of the elaborate antiphon and the solemn form of the chant, accompanied by the incense routine.

The final office of the day was Compline, meaning completion. Whilst ranking as a minor office, along with Prime, Terce, Sext and Nones, it did not take any share in the Psalm 119 recitation. This was because, approaching the dreaded night-time, it was allocated those psalms which spoke of the relevant concerns of darkness, pestilence, evil, watching, peace and rest, namely Psalms 4, 31, 91 and 134. Likewise, the canticle *Nunc dimittis* shared the sentiment of departing in peace.

With the perpetual routine of singing for so many hours each day in an unheated cathedral, it is perhaps not too surprising that short-cuts were tried, and even adopted. It was a peculiarly Sarum custom for the rulers to shorten the psalm antiphon on its announcement. Only the first phrase was sung in order to give the pitch and mode for the psalm which followed immediately. At the end of the psalm and *Gloria Patri*, the antiphon was then sung in full by all.

The lesson readings also suffered cuts, though mainly because of the birth of the breviary, produced for most uses, whereby all the Divine Office was contained in one book, and as its name suggests, brevity was crucial. Some lessons were reduced to a single verse. Sarum Prime had a verse from Zachariah, whilst York chose one from Isaiah; Sarum Compline had a verse from Jeremiah, whilst others used extracts from the Epistles.

Prayers were, of course, a major ingredient in the office. After the psalms, lesson, office hymn and canticle followed the petitions of the *Kyrie*, a remnant of the early litanies, and the Lord's Prayer, usually said privately until the last two phrases when all joined in a responsorial ending. Further versicles and responses led to the collects which followed the pattern used in the mass. The first was the collect for the day, then one for the season, one for the Blessed Virgin Mary as patron, one for the Feast of Relics, peculiar to Sarum because of its extensive collection of holy relics and the devotion and pilgrimages which these promoted, and one for All Saints.

Hymns were referred to in scripture, though not of the type known today. The two earliest non-biblical hymns were from the Greek Church, these being the Trisagion 'Holy God, Holy and mighty, Holy and Immortal, have mercy on us' and the 3rd century 'Hail gladdening light' translated by John Keble. Notwithstanding their eastern popularity, hymns did not gain early recognition in the western Church. A common view was that new, non-scriptural writings were not worthy of recognition in the liturgy of divine worship. However, in its Roman-side-stepping way, the eastern-influenced Gallican Use took on the Trisagion and moulded it into the Good Friday Reproaches which then later appeared in the Sarum Use.

The first notable collector, translator and writer of hymns

was Bishop (Saint) Ambrose in 4th-century Milan. Milan had a strong connection with the early Greek Church, indeed his predecessor, Auxentius, was Greek. Ambrose himself was a scholar of Greek, its literature and drama forms. From these ideas he arranged theological teaching into Latin and in a consistent metrical pattern for easy devotional use. The pattern was a series of four-line verses with rhyming pairs of lines in Iambic tetrameter, that is, four pairs of syllables per line with the emphasis on the second syllable of each pair. Examples of this would be:

Con_ditor_ _alme_ _siderum_ ... or Ve_ni_ Cre_ator_ _Spiritus_ ...

This rhythm suited Latin, though in practice, only a slight stress on syllables 2 and 6 is sufficient to allow a satisfactory flow of plainsong phrases. In modern code, this metre is 8.8.8.8 or Long Metre, which became the standard office hymn format. Even hymns written in later centuries after Ambrose were referred to as Ambrosian because they were written to fit his format, and the ancient melodies which went with this format.

By the ninth century, after earlier work by literature scholar

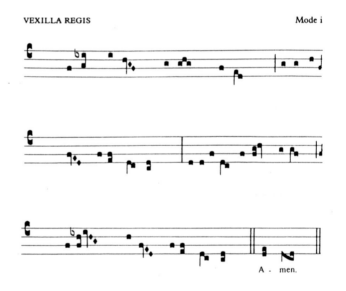

Vexilla regis prodeunt (with acknowledgement to *The New English Hymnal* - number 79), Ambrosian type office hymn in the Dorian mode. The top line of the stave is indicated as Middle C and the note below is legitimately flattened in its two occurrences.

Saint Columba, the Celtic Church had begun to formulate a cycle of hymns for the daily office for weekdays, festivals and seasons. This cycle, comprising hymns mainly of the Ambrosian type, included others of different metre. It was taken up, not only by the Celtic monastic Church, but by Benedictine houses in England, as indicated in a 10th-century hymnal of the monastic Canterbury Cathedral. It must also have been adopted by the Benedictines at Sherborne.

The tunes for these hymns were passed on necessarily by aural tradition, and not committed to a written code until the 10th century. The four-line stave then eventually emerging was able to cover an octave, more than ample for most plainsong melodies. Whilst an indication of Middle C was given in order to show the note relationships in terms of tones and semitones as they fitted into the mode, the actual singing pitch was simply that given by the precentor.

The square nature of plainsong notes originates from the quill pen moving parallel to the stave lines making notes in a series of small dashes. This was a quick and efficient hand-writing method, vital when there was so much demand for music books. Accidentals were not allowed in the modes, except for a flattened B, in all modes, where it was the top note in a rise in a melody. The first and last lines of the melody for *Vexilla regis prodeunt* illustrate this point. The reason for this relaxation was that a semitone at the top was kinder to the ear, if not so modally pure. In the later medieval period, the use of accidentals proliferated, especially through polyphony and organ accompaniment. This necessitated a change in key structure and the demise of the modal system.

Sarum's Hymnal clearly descended from Celtic ancestry, and, through its link to the Ambrosian-influenced Gallican Use, contained many of the earliest office hymns, as did other Celtic descendants such as the hymnals of Exeter and York. The Sarum Hymnal contained some sixty-seven tunes, including alternative tunes to certain hymns used for different seasons. Occasionally, new hymns and tunes were added, both by adoption from other established sources, and by new compositions, some demanded by the recognition of new feast days. Updating and improvement was integral to the management of the Sarum library.

12

DECLINE AND REVIVAL

Following two centuries of growing success and fame at
Sarum, certain influences caused a period of decline which
was also apparent in the Church in general. At the highest level in
the western Christian Church, there was abuse and discord. The
papal schism from 1378 resulted in Europe's Christian countries
dividing their papal loyalties between Rome and Avignon for
forty years. However, abuse and discord had affected the lower
levels of the Church even a century before this.

In contrast to the men of stature and stability in the early
days, the late 13th and early 14th centuries saw men of feeble
contribution and even neglect. In the first hundred years at Old
Sarum there were only three appointments to the bishopric,
whilst in only half that time by the beginning of the 14th
century, there were nine. That represents a rise to six times the
episcopal turnover. Much worse, the first six deans of the 14th
century were all non-resident foreigners, as were four precentors
and three treasurers.[39] These appointments were given by the
Italian popes to their Italian cardinal colleagues who took the
honours, and without doubt, the incomes, but never appeared
at Sarum to undertake duties. Chancellors, archdeacons and
other canons assumed a similar lack of residence and interest,
causing discipline in both worship practice and general lifestyle
to plummet.

Frequent absences of canons in the quire, often resulted in
barely sufficient staff to meet the normal liturgical standards.
The quality of the singing must also have been very doubtful.
However, the few canons who did remain for duty would not
have complained too loudly as they got a greater share of the
undiminished common provisions, and life, if not disciplined,
would have been very comfortable.

One effect of the reduction in canons' attendance was the
rise of the vicars choral or deputies who sang vicariously for the
absent canons. They were clerics, but in minor orders so they
could not assume the full responsibilities or benefits of their
prebendal masters. They, too, were often neglectful of appropriate
behaviour for their cathedral position, and, when discipline

caught up with them, were reprimanded for a multitude of misdemeanours such as arriving late for services, leaving early, chattering in quire, playing ball games in the Close, brawling, entertaining women, for wearing 'a cape of many colours,' a 'belt of marvellous size' and going to Southampton 'in a striped costume.'[38]

Ironically, because the strength of the vicars was in their singing abilities, the musical standard of the cathedral may well have improved. They were certainly the start of an institution which was going to last.

Further neglect was shown in the decline of the colleges of St Nicholas de Vaux and St Edmund's. Chancellor absences and senior clergy lack of interest meant that lecturer posts were left unfilled, and teaching and learning all but disappeared. Sarum's brilliant start in academe had been squandered. Many of the former Oxford scholars drifted back to Oxford and to newly-founded colleges in Cambridge which then became the reliable guardians of the Sarum Use. Scribes, bookbinders and illustrators also found their Sarum trade falling and defected to more flourishing centres such as Cambridge and the newly prosperous wool towns of East Anglia and its trading partner, Flanders.

The decline was not without some effort at reparation. Bishop Mortival decided to revise procedures and regulations, and produced new statutes for the cathedral in 1319. These statutes amended some of the original constitution provisions, and introduced new ones to ensure a firmer regulation of the conduct of canons whether in residential requirements, duties in quire, details of ritual, property management or financial dealings. Not only did this revision pull the cathedral organisation together, but it also pushed the Ordinal, the collation and liturgical over-sight of services, towards the need for a new edition because of the many amendments. It was Precentor Thomas de Welewick in 1342 who produced the new Ordinal, once more providing a revived interest in what was seen as a new Use of Sarum. The statutes ensured a better business control, not least of all by requiring the keeping of Chapter meeting minutes. They also required better care of records and treasured documents, and a senior canon was to be elected annually to the duties of *Custos Munimentorum*.

The facilities for singing boys were greatly enhanced by the formal provision of a boarding school for fourteen pupils with a

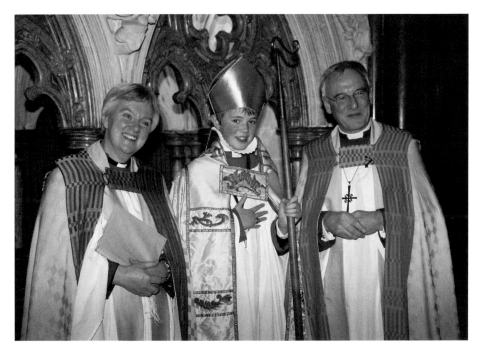

Boy Bishop Joseph Wicks with Dean June Osborne and Lord Bishop David Stancliffe.

master specifically appointed for their teaching. Hitherto there had been no provision for general education, although Osmund had provided for boys to sing in the liturgy, and for associated training to be given by the precentor and chancellor as a small part of their many duties. Endowments to the new boys' school ensured its survival and success. A full, modern education system began to develop and, conversely, quaint medieval charades were abolished.

One of these charades was the boy bishop ceremony, where a boy was elected annually on the December 6 Feast of St Nicholas to act the part of bishop until the post-Christmas Feast of the Holy Innocents. The boy bishop had cope and mitre made to fit, and had boy ministers around him to sing leading parts in services, sitting in superior positions in quire whilst displaced bishop and canons sat in the lower forms. He also delivered a sermon, usually written for him, at an appropriate time, and even gave the pontifical blessing. Great processions were made round the town when the wealthier inhabitants feasted the children with an abundance of sweetmeats.

Bishop Mortival's statutes curtailed the feasting and allowed entertainment of the boys only by canons in the Close. Similar eccentric customs were abolished and more formal care and education of the boys were provided.

The vicars choral became more reliable and increasingly more professional in their singing duties. New vicars had to work a probationary year before acceptance. During that year they had to learn the psalter by heart, though having sung it through 52 times in the process of that year, it would have been no great difficulty. They were then solemnly admitted to their office by the dean.

A common hall of residence was provided for the vicars, and supported by endowments. In 1409 they were chartered by Henry IV as 'The Procurator and Communalty of the Vicars Choral of Salisbury Cathedral,' the procurator being the elected head, usually the organist.[40] Although still appointed and supervised by the dean and chapter, they were given some

This 'south-west prospect' by J. Harris was published about 1715 but is possibly a copy of an earlier view. It shows the bell-tower and the complete library range adjoining the south transept.

measure of self-governance, and even allowed to supplement their corporate endowment income as innkeepers and shop-keepers in the town. Of their body, the six senior members were, from 1443, allowed to attend interviews of potential new entrants along with the dean and elected members of the chapter. By coincidence, six was also the number to which the full complement of fifty-two residential canons, other than the four principals, had dwindled by the time of the Reformation a century later. This number also fixed what was to become the post-Reformation establishment.

Scholastic credibility returned to Sarum with the appointment to the deanery in 1449 of Gilbert Kymer, formerly Chancellor of Oxford University. He procured from Oxford many scholars and scribes, and supervised the building of a library and teaching room above the east cloister. The library was endowed with many historical and theological manuscripts, and teaching, copying and illuminating flourished once more. The 15th century also saw the appointment of a professional singing master to the boys, who also played the organ for services.

A further, major boost to Sarum's recognition came with the canonisation of Osmund in 1457. The many years of reported miracles accredited to Osmund, and the attempted persuasion of successive popes brought eventual success. The setting up of a worthy shrine cost the cathedral much expense, but wealth and fame returned through the visits of many pilgrims to the shrine throughout its 80 years of existence prior to the Reformation.

Perhaps the high point in the return of recognition for Sarum was in the appointment of John Blyth as bishop concurrent with his appointment as Chancellor of Cambridge University from 1494 to 1496. Many immigrant Cambridge scholars, having written treatises defending the purity of the liturgy from the misinterpretations and malpractices of poor Sarum stewardship, regained for Bishop Blyth a cleansed and re-established authority on the Sarum Use.

13

PLAINSONG TO POLYPHONY

As any art develops, it was natural that monophony should eventually take on another dimension. The development of polyphony (Greek: *polyphonos* = many voices), from the 12th century on the continent and from the 14th century in England, was facilitated by two particular factors: the establishment of an efficient method of recording notation on stave lines, and the rise of formal bodies of educated and expert singers.

The first departure from monophodnic plainsong, given its optimum lateral development, was the addition of a second melodic line, parallel or not, but note above note on a plainsong chant. This two–part singing was called 'discant,' a simple form of 'organum.' Organum developed into multi-note flourishes over slower moving notes of a plainsong cantus firmus. Another early form of polyphony was 'conductus,' which comprised two or more parts moving together in identical rhythm. The parts were not usually parallel, nor was there necessarily a plainsong chant base, though it had a practical liturgical use. The purpose of conductus was to conduct the clergy in their processions to a helpful rhythm, not unlike march music of today. A consistent pulse was therefore more important than melodic line. Unlike plainsong chants, this new music ventured into varying note lengths; for instance, alternating long and short notes in triple time became popular. Furthermore, music of such consistent timing and rhythm was convenient material for organ accompaniment and the use of other instruments. From Psalm 150 we know of the long-standing use in worship of trumpet, lute, harp, strings, pipe and 'cymbals.' The latter seems to have been subject to mistranslation in all modern psalters as the original word 'cymbala' referred, not to cymbals but to chiming bells, as any medieval illumination can illustrate. It can be imagined that a general strong sense of rhythm would be imperative to keep together a procession of clergy, a group of singing vicars and two organists.

Experimentation with multiple part-singing was initially restricted to certain, specialist parts of the liturgy. The popular, more congregational ordinary of the mass, and the psalms of the office were left untouched, whilst the more elaborate chants of tropes and antiphons, first referred to as 'anthems' in the Sarum Use, were often set to polyphony for the professional vicars only. Some examples employing high-pitched counter-tenor voices and unusual rhythms caused the notable Old Sarum canon John of Salisbury to write:

> Could you but hear one of these enervating performances executed with all the devices of the art, you might think it a chorus of sirens (ladies) not of men; and you would be astounded by the singers' facility with which indeed neither that of the parrot or nightingale can compare; for this facility is displayed in long passages running up and down, in dividing or in repeating notes (hocket) and phrases, and in clashing together of voices (false relations), while in all this the higher notes are so mingled with the lower that the ears are almost deprived of their power to distinguish[41]

Extreme practices of this kind led Pope John XXII to decree from Avignon in 1322 the forbidding of all but the simplest harmonisation of liturgical chant and the deploring of singers who 'truncate the melodies with hockets, deprave them with discants, and even trope the upper parts with secular songs.'

As in the early *Alleluyas*, before sequences poured words into empty melodic moulds, much early polyphony was, simply, vocalised melodic phrases fitted together. This situation gave rise to a later insertion of words and so was the birth of the motet (French: *mot* = word). Whilst the added words were of spiritual or liturgical origin, the motet form itself came too late to have a formal place in the Sarum liturgy. In the same way, the anthem, as we now know it, is strictly an addition to the reformed office rather than an integral and necessary part of it, albeit the origin of the word is in the term antiphon from the old use.

Polyphonic compositions, in mass or motet form, many of them based on Sarum plainsong themes, flourished in England from the 15th century, and extant works of Dunstable (died 1453), Fayrfax (born 1465) and Taverner (born 1495) still find their way into liturgical music schemes and concert programmes.

The pinnacle of English polyphony was reached, arguably, in the works of Tallis and Byrd at the zenith of the Sarum Use and its transformation into Reformation liturgy. Byrd especially was a conscientious supporter of Sarum Use Catholicism, even through the protestant polarisation of the Reformation. Much of his music was for the Latin mass, the more notable being three mass ordinary settings and gradual proper based anthems in 'Gradualia.'

Polyphonic music necessarily burst out of the straightjacket of the modal system. Artistic license in the frequent use of accidentals brought a new attraction to western ears. New codes of tonal relationships developed into the major and minor keys recognisable today. The Church modes and plainsong had reached the virtual end of their useful life, assisted by the contemporary liturgical changes of the Reformation, and in particular the objection of the protestant reformers to Gregorian music because of its name, being popish and therefore unacceptable.

14

REFORMATION

Henry VIII's interest in changes as mainly domestic and
political; not particularly liturgical and certainly not
doctrinal. It is almost ironical, then, that it was the latter two
aspects which more affected Sarum and the English Church
in general. Even then, the wrath and havoc wreaked upon the
monasteries at the Dissolution from 1536 to 1540 was not
visited on Sarum or other secular churches because they did
not pay direct allegiance to the pope or to parent abbeys outside
England. These latter aspects of the monasteries had long
promoted a bypassing of the English monarch and state in terms
of management, wealth and justice.

As the monasteries were dissolved, so were any connections
with alien houses on the continent, and prebends formerly held
by abbots in Normandy were transferred to English houses or
the Crown. As early as 1490, by orders of Henry VII, the Sarum
prebends of Upavon, Loders and Ogbourne were transferred to
royal Clarendon's Ivychurch Priory, Sion Abbey and the dean
and chapter of Windsor respectively, the latter royal chapel being
in the Sarum Diocese until the Oxford Diocese was formed in
1542. The dissolution of the Ivychurch and Sion houses meant
confiscation of Upavon and Loders by the Crown.

The secular Church did suffer some despoliation, however.
All shrines to saints were suppressed in 1538, and thus the cult of
Saint Osmund was eradicated. His elaborately decorated shrine
in the centre of the Trinity Chapel was dismantled, and only
some time later reappeared in the feeble form of a coffin lid,
now positioned in a dignified memorial. In the same year, Bishop
Nicholas Shaxton, a foremost supporter of the Reformation,
commanded his clergy to send him their treasured relics so that
he might adjudicate on whether or not they were authentic
relics. He asserted that in his diocese:

> ydolatrie hath been practised to vaine things, namely stinking
> boots, mucke combes, lockes of heer, filthy rages and gobbetts
> of wodde (under the name of parcels of the Holy Cross) and
> such pelfrie beyond estimacion; over and besides the shameful
> abuse of such a peradventure be true reliques in dede, whereof
> nevertheless certaine profe is none.[42]

Wyatt's screen, with organ in 1850.

The relics were adjudicated, and most ended up in the town drain. Instructions were also given for the removal of images, stone altars and candles. Decorative altar frontals and vestments were also withdrawn, and plainer dress prevailed.

There were, however, positive sides to Henry VIII's attention to the church. He ordered for the novel use of the vernacular in worship. In 1536, Tyndale's translated Bible was ordered to be used for the reading of all lessons. Latin was still to be the major language, and in the same year, an updated and reformed Sarum

Breviary was published, in Latin but with references to the pope omitted.

The Use of Sarum received its final accolade in 1543 when the Convocation of Canterbury, under Archbishop Thomas Cranmer, formally adopted it for general, obligatory use throughout the southern province. This suppressed the remnants of the uses of Lincoln, Hereford and Bangor, but not that of York which officially, if minimally, survived for another six years in its own, northern province.

Having achieved this large measure of unity in the Church's liturgy, Cranmer then set about translating service material for an extensive use of the vernacular. He started with the processional devotions which preceded the mass, and in 1544, from the Sarum Litany, produced the Litany in English. This then complemented the long-standing practice at Sarum of reciting in English the bidding prayers at the rood screen.

Cranmer continued his enormous task, and in 1548 produced an entirely English Order of the Communion, more or less a translation of the Sarum Missal. He continued with the Divine Office, reducing it to the two services of Matins and Evensong, eliminating the minor offices as well as much of the intricacy of the Sarum rubrics.

In his revised Matins, Cranmer combined the former Matins, Lauds and Prime, consequently including their respective canticles of *Venite*, *Te Deum* and *Benedictus*. In the revised Evensong, so called because he was translating the Sarum and not the Roman or any other use, he combined the former Evensong and Compline and consequently their respective canticles of *Magnificat* and *Nunc dimittis*. Into this format he worked his masterpiece collects, exhortations and rubrics, to contribute to the first English *Book of Common Prayer* published in 1549.

The point of the change to the vernacular was, of course, that worship should be public, and the ordinary, church-going laity should be able to share in it. However, it was acknowledged that in intellectual collegiate establishments, Latin was understood, and indeed commonly used. For such cases, reverse translations of the *Book of Common Prayer* into Latin were authorised. Care had to be taken not to fall into old Latin practices such as a mention of the papal name or other phrases which would conflict with Reformation directions. King Henry VIII himself continued to hear the Latin mass until his death, and his well-educated children, Mary, Elizabeth and Edward, were brought up to be very familiar with it.

Henry had no doctrinal argument with Rome, and readings from an English bible did not conflict with his faith or belief, which was also the official position of the one Holy, Catholic and Apostolic Church. It was the increasing influence of reformers from the continent and the universities after his death which caused the more drastic turning of events. The post-Henrican reduction of the mass from a sacrifice to a memorial service, and its much less frequent use was a major change, not altogether welcomed by many clergy and laity. New Articles of Religion rigidly stated the protestant stance, but the physical removal of roods, images and altars, the focal points of so much devotion, caused considerable distress.

It is not surprising that on the accession of Mary and the return to the old Catholicism, many clergy readily restored roods, images, altars, frontals and vestments which they had secreted instead of destroying.

15

THE *BOOK OF COMMON PRAYER*

In a study of the Sarum Use, the *Book of Common Prayer* is due some attention because of the direct descendancy of the latter from the former. The reverse is also true. The foundation stones of the *BCP* were those of the Sarum Use simply reworked.

With the death of Henry in 1547, Cranmer hastened on with his task of translation and rationalisation, encouraged now by a growing band of reformer-colleagues. The result of his great work came in 1549, at a time, by then, of high religious feelings in both directions. The *Book of Common Prayer* was a simplification of complex forms, and a purging of malpractices and superstitions, along with excesses of decorative literature accumulated over the late medieval years. Apart from the language change, it was to recall the best of early traditions and collate the best liturgical literature into fewer, more practicable services. Under Edward VI the reformers had taken a stronger hold, but the new book was not universally acclaimed to be the long-awaited answer. The vote for its approval by bishops in the House of Lords was as close as ten votes to eight, and many people, clerical and lay, preferred the old ways unchanged.[43] Ironically, many illiterate lay people even preferred the Latin liturgy because of the mystery it sustained, and mystery had been the lifeblood of medieval religion.

Immediately the Prayer Book was issued, Cranmer pursued a way of making it popular with the laity, and asked one of the Court organists, John Merbecke of St George's Royal Chapel at Windsor, to set the ordinary of the Holy Communion to simple music for congregations, defining that there should be only one note per syllable. Merbecke produced his setting, based on Sarum plainsong chants, which was published in the *Praier Boke Noted* (ie with notes) in 1550.

A change was also required in the office music. Plainsong was redundant for musical and political reasons, so the psalms, that vital ingredient of even the reformed office was left without a musical vehicle. The swift result was the rewriting of popular psalms in metrical form and given new tunes, some loosely based on old chants. These were the seeds of the modern hymn. The first collection was by Sternhold, later expanded by Hopkins. In view of his congregational concern, it is remarkable that Cranmer rejected the Latin metrical office hymns as a source, along with the old, unwanted and superfluous material. Hymns, to become the greatest of congregational fare, are not even mentioned in the Prayer Book. Cranmer, of course, was a master of prose, and the translation of the office hymns within the restrictions of metre and rhyme, was a specialism for others. The new metrical psalms had not yet proved their worth.

The publication of the Prayer Book attracted many reformers on the continent, especially Germany and Switzerland and within a couple of years, Cranmer had absorbed further influence from such as Luther, Calvin, Bucer, Martyr and Zwingli. These more extreme protestant views forced a revision to the Prayer Book after only three years, in 1552. Penitential introductions were added to Morning and Evening Prayer (the word 'Evensong' now not used), recitation of the ten commandments added to Holy Communion, and the indulgence of joy in the latter, in the form of *Gloria in excelsis Deo* removed to the end of the service. Notions of the 'real presence' in the words of administration 'The Body of Our Lord...' were changed to 'Take and eat this....' Similarly, the *Benedictus* end of the *Sanctus*, and the *Agnus Dei* were omitted altogether. This meant that some of Merbecke's work was now already redundant.

Academic dress had replaced the glorious vestments of the past. University colleges were, of course, largely ecclesiastical foundations, formerly following the Sarum Use in their chapels, so there were close links. Gowns and hoods became fashionable in the cause of eradicating unworthy ecclesiastical flamboyance, and promoting the better teaching of protestant truth as exemplified in the enlightened universities. The plain Sarum surplice completely replaced the sacramentally tainted alb, and the scarf replaced the stole.

In place of the east-wall stone altar was a free-standing wooden table, without frontal, aligned east-west with the minister standing on the north side facing south so the congregation could see him and the 'cup.' The elements were to be taken kneeling, and the general mood was to be one of internal penitence rather than external splendour.

The pace of reform was moving too fast for some, and hopes for a reversal of the changes were rewarded in the death of Edward in 1553 and the accession of Mary. The *Book of Common Prayer* was repealed and the Latin Sarum Use restored, along with stone

(a) 13th century Sarum Kyrie:

(b) 15th century Sarum Kyrie:

(c) Merbecke's Prayer Book Kyrie:

Merbecke's Communion Service *Kyrie* seen to be derived from a 15th-century Sarum mass which in turn displaced a 13th-century mass.

altars, frontals, vestments, statues and candles. (The royal abbey at Westminster was even re-staffed with monks.) New editions of the (Latin) Breviary and Missal were printed for distribution and obligatory use. Cranmer himself was burned in Oxford, the centre of much of his intellectual support. However, this sea change was short-lived, and with Mary's death in 1558, and the accession of Elizabeth, the reformers took a renewed interest.

However, Elizabeth had been brought up in the Latin tradition, and yet saw the sense in people-friendly worship. She was at once authoritative and democratic. It was important for her not only to balance the two extreme camps, but to steer strongly between them. Within a year of her accession she made a bold attempt to stabilise the Church and its practices in another revision of the Prayer Book. This third book, of 1559, was more moderate and conciliatory. It revised the more puritan book of 1552 to nearer the original of 1549. Vestments and ornaments were allowed again in support of the 1549 recommendations for dress: surplice, scarf and hood for Morning and Evening Prayer, and alb and chasuble or tunicle for Holy Communion. For the latter, where full vestments were not available, the surplice was allowed but the hood was considered inappropriate, partly because of its promotion by protestant partisans, and partly because of its incongruity with traditional Eucharistic vestments which were both more ancient in origin, and of strict liturgical colour.

Prayers and rubrics were altered to the more moderate. The administration words 'The Body of Our Lord...' were restored in front of and in addition to 'Take and eat this....' A prayer for the Queen was added to the Litany, but the petition for deliverance 'from the tyranny of the bishop of Rome and all his detestable enormities' was omitted. The extent of conciliation can be seen in the permission granted in 1560 for a Latin version of the new Prayer Book. This was not, however, a return to the Sarum Use but a strict translation of the current authorised Prayer Book. Sarum did have its own printed edition of that same Latin Prayer Book, but as a learned collegiate institution, it did not need the 1560 permission as authority. Many editions of Sarum's Latin books were printed in Rouen, a notable printing centre on the continent, but also the origin of much 11th-century Norman influence to the Sarum Use, and the capital which Osmund knew well.

At the end of Elizabeth's long and stable reign, the puritans, of extreme reforming ideals, again stirred for greater influence. James I heard their advices and issued the fourth Prayer Book in 1604, though with little puritan consequence other than the abolition of female ministration which had crept into baptismal practice, and the abolition of lesson readings from the Apocrypha. Some prayers were added, and use of the book was made obligatory to the point of excommunication for dissenters who were now a threat of fraction at both extremes. It was also this monarch who ordered a new translation of the Bible, produced in 1611 and known as the King James or Authorised Version.

On the demise of Charles I, the puritan dictatorship banned the Prayer Book along with much of the Church's art and worship accoutrements. A Directory of simple worship was issued, and in liturgical terms, this saw the greatest ever move away from the Sarum Use and the Church's traditions and heritage. Whilst the mid–16th century was drastic in some respects, the mid–17th century was catastrophic in terms of losses of gold and silver valuables, sculptures, paintings, organs, music books and other records, not least of all at Sarum. Mercifully, the depression did not last too long.

The Restoration of Charles II in 1660 inevitably brought a move for the restoration of the Prayer Book, along with another opportunity to revise it. The result was the fifth Prayer Book of 1662, one which retains currency to this day. One natural change was the specifying of the Authorised Version for scripture readings, especially for the Communion epistles and gospels. The psalms, however, where sung or publicly recited, were used in their 1535 Coverdale version, which, through regular and frequent use, had become so familiar. Some changes to rubrics were made, and for the first time, recognition of the high choral tradition was made in the final rubric for Morning and Evening Prayer, namely 'In quires and places where they sing, here followeth the anthem.' Special services were drawn up for the remembrance of King Charles the Martyr and for the restoration of the monarchy which, with other prayers for the State and Parliament, gave a certain glory to the establishment. Unlike the universal appeal and acceptance of the old Sarum liturgy, the rigidity and party bias of the Restoration Prayer Book, which was borne of a royalist reaction to the frugal days of the Commonwealth, to some extent led to a later increase in dissent within the Church and disapproval of its narrow liturgy.

During the 18th century, there was a growing desire for more biblically based expression in worship, and less reliance on liturgical, still less, sacramental worship. The Methodist movement began life through the efforts of Anglican priests Charles and John Wesley. It was five years after John Wesley's death before the movement broke with conformity to the Church of England. Whilst John's strength was in biblical preaching, that of Charles was in his lasting contribution of some 6,500 hymns. The Church of England, however, was slow to adopt them, rigidly upholding the 1698 metrical psalter of Tate and Brady which itself took some time to supersede the 1549 metrical psalms of Sternhold and Hopkins.

During the Church's Victorian revival, well over a hundred

hymnals were produced. The success of *Hymns Ancient and Modern* of 1861 was partly attributed to its inclusion of many ancient office hymns translated from the Latin Sarum Hymnal. The recognition of medieval sources was fashionable at that time when scholars of the high church Oxford Movement sought to revive the best of pre-Reformation practice. Indeed in that same year, the (Latin) Sarum Missal was again published, the first such printing in three centuries. This was largely of and for academic interest although many of the Sarum customs, rituals, music and ornaments were taken up again by churches of the Anglo-Catholic party. The great medieval heritage of plainsong, of which a considerable part survived in spite of the ravages of time and change, was brought to enthusiastic revival, culminating in the founding of the Gregorian Association in 1871, and the Plainsong and Medieval Music Society in 1888.

Whilst new hymnals appeared and the lectionary of lesson readings was revised, there was no attempt to revise the 1662 *Book of Common Prayer*. The Victorian revivalists were concerned more with looking back and rescuing the old rather than with attempting something new.

In America, the 1559 Elizabethan Prayer Book was used as early as 1578 by Frobisher's chaplain, and only a year later by Sir Francis Drake's. The first American Prayer Book was published in 1789, following fairly closely the English one of 1662. It was revised in 1892 and again in 1928.

Whilst the liturgy, in practice, flowered variously in Victorian England without formal revision, there was, parallel with America, a revision in 1928. This book, however, was not approved by Parliament, and as such approval is necessary in England's established Church, it remained an unauthorised and Deposited Prayer Book. Parts of it, however, could be used occasionally with a bishop's consent, and it is through this that the Eucharistic *Benedictus* and *Agnus Dei* came back into use, along with the returning of the *Gloria in excelsis* to the beginning of the mass and after the restored nine-fold *Kyrie*. Composers of the time rushed to add these items to their settings already in use. The liturgy was now nearer to the Sarum Use than it had been since 1549.

During the 1960s and '70s there was official interest again in Prayer Book revision. A Liturgical Commission was set-up and the Commissioners drew upon a wide basis of liturgical practice, not least of all the traditions of the early Christian Church which were the sources for later western uses including that of Sarum. Consideration was given to the preserving of the old English in the 1662 Prayer Book as well as to the use of contemporary language, which in fact all previous Prayer Books had done. Choice was a novel and principal feature of the *Alternative Service Book* of 1980, leading to a variety of sub-rites then used by the Church, not altogether unlike the situation in the middle ages. Since 2000 the two categories of choice have been the still current 1662 *Book of Common Prayer* (supporters of which are not incomparable with the Latin Sarum Use supporters of Cranmer's time), and the revised liturgy in *Common Worship: Services and Prayers for the Church of England*. Accompanying rituals, of course, are still added to taste, and at Sarum many of the ancient traditions have been restored.

16

SARUM TODAY

Old Sarum still shows traces of its long-abandoned castle and cathedral. Their currency was relatively short but they saw a peak in status and power second to none in terms of Church, State and king relationships. More proudly, the present

The cathedral spire as viewed from the cloister. The two-storey stone tower is topped by a 200-foot spire which is the tallest in England.

13th-century cathedral still dominates its begotten city of New Sarum (still its official civic name), a situation becoming increasingly rare in other cathedral cities. The country's tallest spire ensures this continuing dominance, but liturgists will look upon this feature as representative of the many centuries of liturgical dominance.

Of the 13th-century cathedral building, almost all remains today. Two chantry chapels added later respectively north and south of the Trinity chapel, and of different architectural style, were removed in the refurbishments of the architect James Wyatt. The original stone pulpitum screen survives in part in the north-east transept. Most of the transept chapels survive though now not used on a daily basis. The stone altars have gone but the examples of double aumbry remain to the north of the transept and aisle chapels, and double piscinas in the opposite places to the south.

The Close, walled with the king's permission, from stones from the old cathedral, now contains fewer canons than in its early days, but a staff nevertheless fully professional in running the business of the Church in this place, no less significant in its modern way than in times past. Residents of the Close include the bishop and the cathedral's four principal dignitaries; dean, precentor, chancellor and treasurer. Other assistant clergy are also to hand as are several professional lay people such as organists, lay vicars, choristers, teachers, chapter clerk, librarian, vergers, administrators and commercial managers. Part-time volunteers work on rota systems, such as additional cleaners, flower-arrangers, guides and stewards, the latter not unlike the medieval *ostiarius* or doorkeeper. The educational thread remains in the various schools in the Close, though now with little or no direct cathedral control except the cathedral's own school.

The colleges of St Nicholas de Vaux and St Edmund struggled to make the 16th century and were suppressed in 1547. Remnants of the latter survive, more particularly in the form of the church though this is now more of a shell which houses the local arts centre. The St Nicholas Hospital, adjacent to the de Vaux college, survives and thrives on its ancient site, still under the administration of the master, a title continued in many collegiate institutions. A phoenix of the colleges rose in the 19th century in the form of a theological college. This has been replaced by the ecumenical Sarum College, a worthy successor in the continuing tradition.

The Bishop of Sarum's entitlement to be Master of Ceremonies to St Peter's in Rome is only presumed to have ceased at the Reformation, but this is nowhere specified. His office as Provincial Precentor to the Archbishop of Canterbury's College of Bishops remains current, requiring him to commence the singing of '*Veni Creator Spiritus*,' albeit in English, at the consecrations of bishops. Through this he also has an official

A present-day Nativity Crib at the head of the nave where choir processions make a station for adoration and prayer.

place in the enthronement of an Archbishop of Canterbury.

The bishop has two suffragan bishops, happily bearing the historic titles of Ramsbury and Sherborne, who, along with the four archdeacons retain their prebendal stalls in the quire whilst living and working in the areas of their appointment. The archdeaconry titles of Sarum, Wilts and Dorset continue their long history, though Berkshire was allocated to the Oxford diocese in the 16th century, and replaced by a newly created Sherborne archdeaconry in 1836.

A double piscina; one original bowl and one destroyed.

The residentiary canons, these now being limited to the four principals, have residentiary duties by rota, and there is a complement of canons now holding this style and title '*honoris causa*,' with stalls in the quire for use on special occasions, but usually with pastoral livings in diocesan parishes. Whilst the prebendal titles nominally remain, the properties and rights of income have long been disposed of or reorganised in accordance with modern employment practice. The Confraternity of Benefactors, first established in 1389 for distinguished service to or representation of the cathedral, has recently been revived and continues in its ancient purpose.

The Advent Procession (exit).

The professional lay vicars and organists have replaced the early medieval quire canons and their *rectores chori* or rulers, other than the residentiaries, for the singing of the daily office, the singing now restricted to Evening Prayer or Evensong as the Church in general once more follows Sarum in calling it. The Eucharist employs some of the old traditions with crucifer, acolytes with tapers, incense thurifer on feast days, celebrant, deacon and sub-deacon with text held in high respect. Vestments are largely of the present-day colour code, and unlike early Sarum days, the laity now play a large part in the Eucharist.

Quire robes retain some similarities with their antecedents. The fur-lined *pellicium* has now given way to the more slender cassock, traditionally black for the Church in general and scarlet for appointments and foundations of royal origin. Sarum cassocks have been traditionally double-breasted, where Roman cassocks are single and multi-buttoned. The colour of Sarum cassocks has changed in modern times to a shade of green matching a prominent colour in the cathedral's interior decor. The long white Sarum surplice continues in use, though the alb has returned for sanctuary use. The black cloak is now used only out of doors, or in extremely cold spells.

The hood of the ancient almuce or shoulder cape gained new life at the Reformation in the colours of the appropriate university, black lined with crimson for Oxford, and black lined with white for Cambridge. In Georgian times, it was elongated to allow it to pass over the large, fashionable wigs, which accounts for its now hanging down the back rather than resting on the shoulders. It is used for the office though not for the eucharist. Sadly the ancient hood of Sarum canons, in reddish-brown calabre, and that of the principals in grey and white fur did not survive because the cathedral's collegiate foundations failed to bloom into university colleges which were the only institutions to continue the medieval hood tradition.

The former manner of reverence, the *inclinatus* or Sarum bow survives more widely now than the Roman genuflexion. It is still accorded by the canons to the dean, or to the bishop, as they leave the quire, east or west respectively, in the entry and exit processions, which, of course, are a relatively modern idea. Processions in the older sense are not so common but perhaps more comprehensive. The simplest of modern-day processions are those to the Trinity Chapel on the feast of Saint Osmund and feasts of the Blessed Virgin Mary.

The nearest approach to the ancient tradition is the pre-Eucharist procession on Sundays in Lent, when the clergy and choir process singing Cranmer's revision of the Sarum Litany. The Good Friday rites revive the ancient Creeping to the Cross, Sarum once more showing its Gallican parenthood. Sarum's great Palm Sunday procession has been revived in modest scale, the town-wide procession being dropped as has the parading of the reserved sacrament. Although the altars are not sprinkled during processions, at Eastertide, the procession makes a station at the Easter Garden instead of the rood screen, and in Christmastide, at the Nativity Scene.

Much more complex is the modern-day Advent Procession. In this case, the procession is the whole service, consisting of two choirs moving from west to east, with several stations for readings, carols, and the ancient pre-Christmas *Magnificat* antiphons, and with increasing candle light indicating the passing from the darkness of original sin to the pre-Christmas promise of redemption. Similarly the Epiphany Procession is an elaborate illustration of the kings' gifts at the manger.

Of the Sarum Lenten Veil, formerly suspended in the presbytery during Lent, there remains only the windlass used for raising the fabric, attached to a pillar at the north side of the presbytery step. The dramatic representations of the instruments of the Passion formerly embroidered on the Veil are now to be seen in the modern altar frontal of natural, undyed colour and matching vestments.

Notwithstanding Cranmer's merging of Evensong and Compline, the late evening office of Compline has been revived, in English of course, complete with the Sarum chants and antiphons. Although no ritual is involved, and excluding the antiphon *Salve Regina* which always ended the medieval service, Compline is probably the nearest approach to the ancient daily liturgy at Sarum as is possible.

The people's Eucharist book now keeps the congregation in touch with the altar missal in use. Instead of an abundance of rubrics, the Eucharist book has additional, helpful devotions and quotations from various Christian sources. A separate hymn book is now essential, allowing congregational participation at places where the medieval canons would have sung plainsong propers. Of the hymns sung today, most are of post-Reformation composition, including samples of Charles Wesley, along with those of Victorian and contemporary writers, including former precentors and current precentor of Sarum. Balancing these are some of the ancient Sarum office hymns set to their traditional plainsong tunes. Post-Reformation Anglican chant is now the norm for the choir's singing of the psalms in the daily routine of the monthly cycle as directed by Cranmer.

That which might appear to be relatively new in the revised liturgy currently in use, such as the Kiss of Peace, lay procession of the Eucharistic elements, deacon's dismissal, and even a nave altar, in fact have direct links back to the Sarum Use. As long as public worship continues, so will the development of its liturgical forms, seeking ancient roots yet contemporary validity. The continuing revivals of old liturgy at Salisbury are not mere historical spectacles; they are useful symbols and vehicles of devotion, using ancient materials as does the very structure of the building, for both the regular congregation and pilgrim visitors alike.

A novel 20th-century development at Sarum was the addition of the girls' choir to the choral foundation. Whilst new and bold in its particular concept, it complements the pioneering of Sarum's early liturgists as well as the enlightenment of modern society. It would be fair to note that Sarum's fellow cathedrals at York, Lincoln, Hereford, Bangor and elsewhere, though united now in common liturgies, preserve something of their own character and also constantly strive to maintain the high standards of their ancestors. The Church's Liturgical Commission also works, as did early Sarum, for the review and updating of material to maintain helpful forms of worship.

It is fitting to recall what Bishop Giles de Bridport said 750 years ago:

> Among the churches of the whole world, the Church of Sarum hath shone resplendent, like the sun in his full orb, in respect of its divine service and its ministers.[44]

Bishop Giles officiated at the consecration in 1258, and the clean, new Chilmark stone of the walls, as well as the liturgy within, must have prompted his long-beloved metaphor, still relevant today.

APPENDIX

The Ordinary of the Mass

Reprinted from the *Graduale Sarisburiense*
by W. H. Frere (1894)

(MS H.1.c – by permission of the British Library)

facsimile copies of a 13th–century document

NOTES

1. F.M. Stenton, *Anglo-Saxon England* (Oxford, 1971), p. 130.
2. F.T. Bergh, 'Sarum Rite' in *The Catholic Encyclopedia* (New York, 1912).
3. J.R.H. Moorman, *A History of the Church in England* (London, 1963), p. 30.
4. Stenton (n. 1), p. 183.
5. D. Greenway: *Fasti Ecclesiae Anglicanae, 1066-1300,* vol. 4 (Salisbury) (London 1991).
6. *The Anglo-Saxon Chronicles* for 1086, (A. Savage, translator), (London 1982).
7. D. Greenway, 'The False *Institutio* of St Osmund' in D. Greenway, C. Holdsworth & J. Sayers (editors), *Tradition and Change* (Cambridge, 2002), p. 79.
8. D. Greenway, *Orders and Rank at Old Sarum* (London, 1991), p. 57.
9. *The Anglo-Saxon Chronicles* (n. 6) for 1123.
10. K. Edwards, 'Salisbury Cathedral – An Ecclesiastical History' in *The Victoria History of Wiltshire*, vol. 3 (London, 1956), p. 160.
11. D. M. Hope, 'Liturgical Books' in C. Jones, Cheslyn, G. Wainwright & E. Yarnold (editors), *The Study of Liturgy* (London, 1978), p. 78.
12. W.H. Frere, *Sarum Use*, vol. 1 (Cambridge, 1898), p. 328.
13. Greenway (n. 7), p. 78.
14. Frere (n. 12), p. xix.
15. C. Wordsworth, *Salisbury Processions and Ceremonies* (Cambridge 1901), p. 121
16. Frere (n. 12), p. xxvii.
17. T. Webber, *Scribes and Scholars at Salisbury Cathedral c. 1075-1125* (New York, 1992).
18. Wordsworth (n. 15), preface.
19. Frere (n.12), p. xxiii.
20. Ibid., vol. 2, p. xxii.
21. Greenway (n. 5).
22. Frere (n. 12), vol. 2, p. xxii.
23. Wordsworth (n. 15), p. 122.
24. D. Rock, *The Church of Our Fathers*, vol. 4 (London, 1852), p. 54.
25. Greenway (n. 8), p. 59.
26. Wordsworth (n. 15), p. 108.

27. Ibid., p. 109.
28. Rock (n. 24), vol. 2, p. 133.
29. Ibid., p. 223.
30. Edwards: p160.
31. Rock (n. 24), vol. 4, p. 235.
32. Ibid., p. 270.
33. Wordsworth (n. 15), p. 74.
34. E. Dufffy, *The Stripping of the Altars* (London, 1992), p. 23.
35. P.G. Cobb, 'The Liturgy of the Word in the Early Church' in C. Jones etc. (n. 11), p. 185.
36. Ibid., p. 183.
37. Ibid.
38. Edwards (n. 10), p. 170.
39. Ibid., p. 173.
40. Ibid., p. 179.
41. D. Stevens, *The Pelican History of Music* (Harmondsworth, 1982), p. 235.
42. Wordsworth (n. 15), p. 40.
43. P. Dearmer, *The Story of the Prayer Book* (Oxford, 1933), p.53.
44. Wordsworth (n. 15), preface.

BIBLIOGRAPHY

G. Dix, *The Shape of the Liturgy* (London, 1945).

E. Duffy, *The Stripping of the Altars* (London, 1992).

K. Edwards, 'Salisbury Cathedral – An Ecclesiastical History' in *The Victoria History of Wiltshire*, vol. 3 (London, 1956).

S.H. Evans, *Salisbury Cathedral – A Reflective Guide* (Salisbury, 1985).

J. Harper, *The Forms and Orders of Western Liturgy from the 10th to the 18th Century* (Oxford, 1991).

K. Hylson-Smith, *Christianity in England from Roman Times to the Reformation* (London, 1999).

C. Jones, Cheslyn, G. Wainwright & E. Yarnold (editors), *The Study of Liturgy* (London, 1978).

N. Sandon, *The Use of Salisbury* (Newton Abbot, 1984).

R. Spring, *Salisbury Cathedral – A Landmark in England's Heritage* (Salisbury, 1991).